Welcome to the crazy, money-making world of sales! You see, selling isn't just about peddling stuff like a pushy door-to-door salesperson. Oh no, it's way cooler than that! In this book, we're going to unravel the secrets of sales and how to become a value-adding ninja!

Picture this: sales is like solving a puzzle, but instead of finding that pesky missing piece under the couch, we're hunting for what our customers truly crave. It's all about understanding their needs and desires, and then BOOM! Offering them solutions that'll rock their socks off!

Forget the cheesy sales tactics and desperate pleas. We're all about becoming trusted advisors here! So, grab your cape, because we're embarking on a heroic mission to listen, ask questions, and empathize with our customers. Holy sales strategy, Batman!

Adding value is our superpower! It's like Batman's utility belt, but instead of grappling hooks, we've got knowledge about industry trends and customer feedback. The more we know, the better we can serve our customers and save the day!

Now, let's talk money, honey! Money is just a fancy system of value in the economy. So, how do we rake in the big bucks? Simple as pie - we add loads of value to every single sale! The more value we bring, the more money we make. Ka-ching!

So, get ready to rock the sales world with our value-packed approach. From building epic connections to tackling pesky objections, we're going to arm you with the most incredible sales strategies ever! Time to level up your sales game and unleash the power of adding value!

Now, who's ready to be a sales superstar? Let's do this!

1.   Introduction: The Art of Sales

The Importance of Sales

Evolution of Sales in Today's Market

2.   Understanding Sales Fundamentals

Sales Process Overview

Types of Sales: B2B, B2C, Direct, Indirect

3.   Effective Communication and Interpersonal Skills

The Power of Communication in Sales

Active Listening and Building Rapport

Nonverbal Communication and Body Language

4.   Prospecting and Lead Generation

Identifying Target Audience and Ideal Customer Profile

Prospecting Methods: Cold Calling, Networking, Referrals, etc.

Utilizing Technology for Lead Generation

5.   Creating Compelling Sales Presentations

Crafting a Persuasive Sales Pitch

Developing Engaging Visuals and Storytelling

Addressing Customer Needs and Pain Points

6.   Negotiation and Closing Techniques

Understanding Negotiation Dynamics

Overcoming Objections and Handling Rejections

Strategies for Effective Closing

7. Building and Managing Customer Relationships

Importance of Relationship-Building in Sales

Customer Lifecycle Management

Providing Exceptional Customer Service

8. Utilizing Technology in Sales

CRM Systems and Sales Automation

Social Media for Sales and Personal Branding

Virtual Selling and Online Platforms

9. Sales Ethics and Professionalism

Maintaining Ethical Standards in Sales

Transparency and Honesty in Customer Interactions

Long-Term Relationship Building vs. Short-Term Gains

10. Sales Metrics and Performance Measurement

Key Performance Indicators (KPIs) in Sales

Evaluating Sales Performance and Goal Setting

Continuous Improvement and Learning

11. Adapting to Different Selling Environments

B2B vs. B2C Sales Strategies

Inside Sales vs. Field Sales

Navigating Global and Cross-Cultural Sales

12. Time Management and Productivity in Sales

Planning and Organizing Sales Activities

Efficiently Managing Leads and Opportunities

Balancing Sales and Administrative Tasks

13. Sales Leadership and Team Management

Transitioning from Salesperson to Sales Manager

Motivating and Leading Sales Teams

Coaching and Developing Sales Talent

14. Managing Sales Challenges

Handling Sales Burnout and Rejection

Dealing with Price Objections and Competition

Adapting to Market Changes and Industry Trends

15. Future of Sales and Emerging Trends

AI and Automation in Sales

Personalization and Customer-Centric Selling

Predictive Analytics and Data-Driven Sales

16. Conclusion: Mastering the Art of Sales

Recap of Key Takeaways

Chapter 1: Embracing the Journey: The Art of Sales

Welcome to a world where every interaction is an opportunity, every conversation is a canvas, and every challenge is a chance to shine. This chapter marks the beginning of your voyage into the captivating realm of sales—an art form where your enthusiasm, creativity, and determination will paint a masterpiece of success.

Unveiling the Magic of Sales: Imagine stepping onto a stage where you are both the artist and the conductor. Sales isn't just about products and services; it's about weaving dreams, building connections, and making an impact. Every sale is a collaboration, a dance of ideas, needs, and solutions.

A Symphony of Human Connection: At its core, sales is about connecting with people. Whether you're working in a bustling marketplace or engaging across digital landscapes, remember that you're not just selling—you're connecting. You're providing solutions, fulfilling desires, and brightening the lives of those you engage with.

Fuelling Your Passion: Think of sales as the adventure of a lifetime. It's a chance to explore different industries, to learn about the nuances of human behaviour, and to constantly challenge yourself to reach new heights. Your passion is your greatest asset; let it guide you, inspire you, and fuel your drive.

Embracing Rejections as Steppingstones: In the world of sales, rejections are not roadblocks; they are steppingstones. Each "no" brings you closer to a "yes." Every rejection is an opportunity to learn, adapt, and grow. Remember, every successful salesperson has faced rejection—it's how you bounce back that truly defines you.

Crafting Your Own Story: You are the storyteller of your sales journey. Your experiences, triumphs, and even setbacks shape your narrative. Your dedication to your craft will echo through your interactions, creating a legacy of trust and excellence.

Embodying Empathy and Empowerment: The art of sales is not just about persuasion; it's about empathy. Understanding the needs and desires of your customers allows you to offer solutions that truly resonate. Your genuine care and consideration empower your clients to make informed decisions that better their lives.

Unleashing Your Creativity: Sales is your canvas, and your strategies are your brushstrokes. Get creative! Experiment with new approaches, explore fresh perspectives, and innovate in your interactions. The most memorable salespeople are those who dare to think outside the box.

Celebrating Small Victories: In the intricate tapestry of sales, every thread counts. Celebrate each connection you make, every deal you close, and every milestone you achieve. Small victories are the steppingstones to monumental success.

Embracing the Continuous Journey: Remember, the art of sales is a lifelong journey of growth and self-discovery. As you venture forward, you'll refine your techniques, expand your horizons, and touch countless lives. Be open to learning, and let each experience enrich your artistry.

Conclusion: Your Canvass Awaits As you embark on this exhilarating journey into the art of sales, remember that every challenge you face is an opportunity to become a better, more refined artist. Your canvas awaits your touch, your energy, and your passion. Embrace the intricacies, embrace the joy, and embrace the profound impact you have on the world through the art of sales. Let your journey be one of boundless enthusiasm, growth, and fulfilment.

The Symphony of Commerce: The Importance of Sales

In the grand orchestra of business, sales takes centre stage as the conductor that orchestrates the harmonious exchange between value and desire. As we delve into the heart of this symphony, we uncover the profound significance of sales—the driving force that propels economies, fosters innovation, and fulfils the dreams of both consumers and creators.

Fuelling Economic Engines: Sales isn't just about transactions; it's the engine that fuels economies around the globe. From the local bakery to multinational corporations, every business thrives on the energy of sales. The revenue generated flows back into communities, supporting jobs, services, and growth.

Bridging Dreams and Reality: Behind every product or service lies a dream waiting to be fulfilled. Sales bridges the gap between aspiration and achievement. It transforms an idea into a tangible reality that can enhance lives, solve problems, and open new horizons. Without sales, these dreams remain dormant.

Fostering Innovation: Innovation and sales are intertwined like the melodies of a well-composed sonata. The pursuit of sales encourages businesses to constantly innovate—to develop better solutions, create captivating experiences, and adapt to the evolving needs of the world. Sales drives the cycle of improvement, pushing industries to reach new heights.

Creating Transformative Experiences: Sales isn't a mere transaction; it's an experience. A skilled salesperson crafts a journey where every touchpoint resonates with the customer's desires and needs. It's about creating an emotional connection, making the customer feel valued, and leaving an indelible mark on their memory.

Empowering Individuals and Businesses: Sales is empowerment in action. It empowers individuals to discover solutions that enrich their lives. It empowers businesses to showcase their value and contribute to the greater good. Through sales, possibilities unfold, relationships flourish, and growth becomes attainable.

Building Enduring Relationships: Sales is the genesis of relationships that endure beyond transactions. Trust, integrity, and authenticity are the cornerstones of these relationships. A successful salesperson nurtures bonds that transform customers into advocates, creating a ripple effect that amplifies the impact of their influence.

Fuelling Progress and Evolution: Sales propels progress and evolution, pushing industries forward in the journey of advancement. The pursuit of growth fosters healthy competition, encourages investment in research and development, and drives industries to evolve in response to changing landscapes.

Conclusion: The Conductor of Transformation As we peel back the layers of commerce, the importance of sales becomes vividly clear. It's not just a function; it's a catalyst for transformation. It's a driving force that transforms ideas into realities, aspirations into accomplishments, and connections into enduring relationships. The symphony of commerce wouldn't be complete without the resonating melodies of sales—the conductor that shapes the rhythm of business, transforming aspirations into harmonious realities.

Reshaping Horizons: The Evolution of Sales in Today's Market

In the ever-shifting landscape of modern commerce, the evolution of sales has carved a path of transformation that's as exhilarating as it is impactful. As we step into this dynamic arena, we witness the metamorphosis of sales, driven by technological advancements, changing consumer behaviours, and a new era of personalized engagement.

The Technological Revolution: Technology has unfurled a new canvas for sales—a canvas where algorithms analyse data, automation streamlines processes, and artificial intelligence predicts trends. From CRM systems that manage relationships to predictive analytics that guide decisions, technology has become a formidable ally in the modern salesperson's toolkit.

From Transactions to Relationships: The evolution of sales isn't just about moving products; it's about building relationships. The transactional nature of sales has given way to a relationship-centric approach. Today's sales professionals are curators of experiences, crafting personalized journeys that resonate with the customer's values and needs.

The Power of Data-Driven Insights: In this age, sales isn't just about intuition; it's about informed decision-making. Data-driven insights provide a panoramic view of consumer behaviours, preferences, and pain points. Armed with this knowledge, sales professionals can tailor their strategies to meet the precise needs of their audience.

Personalization: The North Star: In a world inundated with choices, personalization is the lodestar that guides successful sales endeavours. Today's customers expect tailor-made experiences that cater to their unique tastes. Sales professionals adept at curating personalized solutions have an edge in forging meaningful connections.

Omnichannel Engagement: Gone are the days of a single touchpoint. The evolution of sales has ushered in an era of omnichannel engagement. From social media to websites, email to in-person interactions, customers expect a seamless journey across multiple platforms.

Value-Centric Selling: Today's customers aren't just looking for products; they're seeking value. Sales professionals who focus on articulating the value their offerings bring to the table are the ones who resonate most with the modern consumer.

Sustainability and Social Impact: In a socially conscious age, sales has embraced a role in shaping a better world. Companies that align with sustainability and social impact initiatives not only attract customers but also contribute to a greater cause.

Embracing Agility and Adaptability: The modern salesperson is a chameleon, adapting to shifting market dynamics. Agility and adaptability are the traits that define successful sales professionals, allowing them to navigate the tides of change with finesse.

Conclusion: A New Horizon of Opportunity The evolution of sales has brought about a new horizon of opportunity—a horizon where technology empowers, personalization resonates, and relationships thrive. As we navigate this transformative landscape, we recognize that the essence of sales remains unchanged: it's about understanding, connecting, and fulfilling needs. The canvas may have transformed, but the art of sales, with all its nuances and melodies, continues to shape the symphony of commerce in ways that inspire, engage, and delight.

Chapter 2: Unveiling the Tapestry: Understanding Sales Fundamentals

Amid the dynamic realm of sales, where strategies may evolve and technologies may shift, one truth remains unwavering: the importance of understanding sales fundamentals. In this chapter, we embark on a journey of discovery, unravelling the threads that compose the very foundation of successful salesmanship.

The Essence of Sales: At the heart of it all, sales is about connection. It's about the art of weaving a narrative that resonates with hearts and minds. By understanding this essence, we step onto a path where genuine interactions supersede scripted pitches.

Customer-Centric Approach: The compass of sales points resolutely to the customer. It's about understanding their desires, pain points, and aspirations. When we embrace this customer-centric perspective, every interaction becomes an opportunity to serve, enrich, and exceed expectations.

The Power of Listening: In the tapestry of sales, the thread of listening holds unparalleled significance. When we truly listen, we unearth insights that illuminate the path to solutions. It's in these silent moments of understanding that relationships begin to flourish.

Effective Communication: Communication is the loom on which sales is woven. The words we choose, the tone we adopt, and the empathy we convey—they all contribute to the artistry of effective communication that leaves an indelible mark.

Building Trust: Trust is the golden thread that binds successful sales interactions. When customers believe in the authenticity of our intentions and the value we offer, trust blossoms, forming the cornerstone of lasting relationships.

Product Knowledge: The fabric of sales is interwoven with the threads of knowledge. Thorough understanding of the products or services we offer allows us to articulate value, answer questions, and provide solutions with confidence.

Overcoming Objections: Objections are but knots in the tapestry of sales. By addressing objections with empathy, providing solutions, and conveying understanding, we untangle the knots and continue weaving the story.

Closing the Deal: The climax of the sales journey—the moment of closure. When we approach this juncture with honesty, enthusiasm, and genuine concern for the customer's needs, we sew the final stitches of trust and commitment.

Adapting and Innovating: Just as threads must be adjusted to create intricate patterns, successful salespeople must adapt to the ever-changing landscape. Embracing innovation and keeping pace with market shifts ensures the tapestry remains relevant and vibrant.

Conclusion: The Masterpiece of Fundamentals Understanding sales fundamentals isn't just about mastering a set of skills; it's about co-creating a masterpiece with each interaction. It's about weaving connections, nurturing relationships, and enriching lives. As we delve into these fundamental truths, we step into the vibrant realm of sales, equipped not only with techniques but also with a profound appreciation for the artistry that underpins every successful sales endeavour.

Unfolding the Symphony: Sales Process Overview

Like a beautifully composed symphony, the sales process orchestrates harmonious interactions that lead to success. In this section, we embark on a journey through the stages of the sales process, each note contributing to the melodious progression towards achieving our goals.

Stage 1: Prospecting and Discovery The first note in our symphony is the art of prospecting. This is where the spotlight shines on identifying potential customers who align with our offerings. Just as a composer carefully selects the instruments for a piece, we meticulously target those who resonate with our product or service. Discovery is the interlude where we delve deep into understanding their needs, challenges, and aspirations. It's the foundation upon which the rest of the symphony is built.

Stage 2: Building Rapport and Trust As our symphony progresses, the notes of building rapport and trust take centre stage. Just as a musical ensemble tunes in perfect harmony, we strike a chord of genuine connection with our prospects. We listen, understand, and empathize, creating an atmosphere where trust can flourish. This connection lays the groundwork for a melody of partnership.

Stage 3: Presenting Value and Solutions Now, the spotlight turns to presenting value and solutions—a crescendo of knowledge, enthusiasm, and tailored offerings. Just as a musician showcases their virtuosity, we demonstrate how our product or service addresses the specific needs and aspirations of our prospects. This is where our symphony reaches its most captivating height.

Stage 4: Addressing Concerns and Objections Every symphony encounters moments of tension and resolution. Similarly, in sales, addressing concerns and objections is the bridge that leads us to harmony. We listen attentively, respond empathetically, and weave the threads of understanding to untangle any doubts. This stage transforms objections into opportunities, like a skilful musician transforming dissonance into melody.

Stage 5: Closing the Deal As our symphony approaches its finale, we step into the spotlight of closing the deal. With confidence and sincerity, we guide our prospects towards the final notes of commitment. The closing stage is where every note, every interaction, culminates in the decisive moment that marks the completion of a harmonious journey.

Stage 6: Follow-Up and Nurturing Yet, our symphony doesn't end with the final chord. It echoes through the follow-up and nurturing stage—a refrain of care and dedication. Just as a musical composition lingers in the minds of its listeners, we ensure that our customers continue to feel valued and supported. This nurturing stage paves the way for future crescendos of collaboration.

Conclusion: The Symphony Continues The sales process is a symphony—a masterpiece of strategic movements, genuine connections, and harmonious interactions. As we journey through the stages, we play each note with intention and skill, crafting a melody that resonates with our prospects. With this process as our guide, we compose success, creating a symphony that echoes not just in the moment of closure but throughout the harmonious relationship we build with our customers.

Unveiling the Melodies: Types of Sales

Just as a symphony is composed of various instruments, the world of sales resonates with different types, each playing its unique melody. In this section, we explore the diverse harmonies of sales, from B2B to B2C, and the intriguing dance of direct and indirect approaches.

B2B (Business-to-Business): Creating Corporate Symphonies in the B2B realm, the symphony unfolds on a grand stage of collaboration between businesses. Like two orchestras harmonizing to create a masterpiece, companies engage in intricate partnerships. This type of sales showcases the art of understanding the needs, challenges, and aspirations of fellow enterprises. The melodies here are composed of complex negotiations, strategic alignments, and solutions that amplify success across the business landscape.

B2C (Business-to-Consumer): Crafting Individual Crescendos B2C sales carry the essence of a soloist captivating an audience. Here, the symphony is tailored to resonate with the desires and emotions of individual consumers. Just as a musician expresses the heart of a composition, B2C sales masterfully present products and services that align with personal aspirations. The melodies in this realm are filled with storytelling, emotional connections, and the art of satisfying the unique preferences of each customer.

Direct Sales: The Solo Performance In the realm of direct sales, the focus is on one-on-one connections. It's like a solo musician engaging intimately with their audience. This approach involves personal interactions, where the salesperson is both composer and performer. The melodies here are characterized by persuasive communication, relationship-building, and the art of converting a potential lead into a satisfied customer.

Indirect Sales: The Orchestra's Crescendo Indirect sales, on the other hand, are like an orchestral composition with multiple instruments playing in harmony. This type involves utilizing intermediaries such as distributors, retailers, or affiliates to reach customers. Each intermediary plays a unique part, contributing to the harmonious whole. The melodies in this realm are built upon partnerships, effective communication with intermediaries, and orchestrating the entire ecosystem to create a melodious journey to the end customer.

Conclusion: A Symphony of Sales In the world of sales, the types are the different movements of a symphony—a symphony that resonates with the needs, desires, and preferences of various audiences. B2B and B2C, direct and indirect—each type is a melody that requires a skilled conductor to bring out its beauty. Just as a symphony is most captivating when it incorporates a variety of instruments, successful sales strategies often embrace a harmonious blend of these types, creating a rich and vibrant composition that strikes the chords of success in the hearts of customers.

Chapter 3. Harmonizing Connections: Effective Communication and Interpersonal Skills

Welcome to the heart of our symphony—where the art of communication and the magic of interpersonal skills take centre stage. Just as musicians communicate through their instruments, sales professionals communicate through the power of words, empathy, and connection. In this section, we explore how to create harmonious interactions that resonate with clients and lead to beautiful symphonies of success.

The Dance of Words: Communication Mastery Effective communication is the melody that guides every successful sales interaction. It's the conductor's baton, guiding the rhythm of the conversation. Just as a skilled musician knows when to play softly and when to crescendo, a salesperson understands the importance of choosing words that resonate with the client's needs. The melodies here are formed through active listening, clear articulation, and the ability to convey complex ideas with simplicity and grace.

Empathy: The Bridge of Connection Empathy is the bridge that connects two souls, just as a musical bridge unites different parts of a composition. When a salesperson listens with genuine care, they understand the client's challenges, dreams, and aspirations. This understanding creates a symphony of trust and rapport. The melodies in this realm are composed of emotional intelligence, the art of putting oneself in another's shoes, and the ability to respond with kindness and understanding.

Nonverbal Communication: The Unspoken Harmony Just as the silence between notes in music holds significance, so does nonverbal communication in sales. A smile, a confident handshake, or a nod—all contribute to the symphony of connection. Just as a conductor's gestures guide the orchestra, a salesperson's body language and facial expressions convey confidence and sincerity. The melodies here are composed of eye contact, posture, and gestures that harmonize with the spoken word.

Adaptability: The Improvisation of Sales In music, improvisation adds a unique touch to a performance. Similarly, adaptability is the art of improvising within sales interactions. Just as a jazz musician responds to the flow of a composition, a salesperson adjusts their approach based on the client's reactions. The melodies in this realm are shaped by the ability to pivot, the art of addressing unexpected questions, and the grace of steering the conversation towards mutual understanding.

Conclusion: A Symphony of Connection Effective communication and interpersonal skills are the essence of creating beautiful symphonies within sales. Just as musicians harmonize their instruments, sales professionals harmonize their words, empathy, and presence to create an unforgettable experience for clients. When communication is a melody that resonates with truth and compassion, and interpersonal skills are the rhythm that fosters trust, the result is a symphony of success that echoes in the hearts of both the salesperson and the client.

The Resonance of Success: The Power of Communication in Sales

Welcome to a world where words become instruments of success, and communication takes centre stage as the driving force behind every triumph. Imagine a symphony of words, carefully orchestrated to create harmony, build trust, and inspire action. In this section, we delve into the profound impact of communication, revealing how it shapes the narrative of sales and crafts melodies of achievement.

The Language of Connection Communication is more than just words; it's the conduit through which relationships are formed. Just as a conductor unites musicians to play in perfect harmony, effective communication bridges the gap between the salesperson and the client. It's about speaking the language of connection, where each sentence resonates with authenticity and respect, creating a melody that sparks understanding.

Empathy's Transformative Melody Empathy is the secret ingredient that infuses communication with soul. Just as a ballad evokes emotions, empathy stirs feelings of genuine care and consideration. When a salesperson truly listens and understands a client's needs, their words become a comforting melody that acknowledges and addresses those needs. Empathy makes communication a dance of understanding, where every word carries the weight of authenticity.

Influence Through Narratives Just as a masterful storyteller captivates their audience, a skilled salesperson weaves narratives that captivate clients. The power of storytelling turns features into meaningful benefits and objections into opportunities. It's about crafting narratives that resonate with the client's journey, desires, and aspirations. These stories become a symphony of persuasion, playing on the strings of emotion and logic.

Building Bridges Through Clarity Clear communication is the foundation upon which successful interactions are built. Just as a clear melody stands out in a composition, clear communication stands out in a crowded marketplace. It's about distilling complex ideas into simple, resonant messages that echo in the minds of clients. Clarity transforms communication into a melodic conversation, were understanding flows effortlessly.

Conclusion: A Symphony of Success Communication is the conductor's wand that directs the sales orchestra towards success. It's the grand crescendo that leads to closed deals, satisfied clients, and fulfilled aspirations. When words are wielded with empathy, influence, and clarity, they create a symphony of trust, rapport, and achievement. As a salesperson, you hold the baton to this orchestration, crafting melodies of triumph that resonate not only in the realm of sales but also in the hearts of those you serve.

The Harmony of Connection: Active Listening and Building Rapport

Step into a world where conversations are not just exchanges of words, but a dance of understanding and resonance. Imagine a melody of dialogue where each note is carefully played, creating a rhythm of connection. In this section, we explore the transformative powers of active listening and the art of building rapport, where conversations become harmonious symphonies of engagement.

The Art of Active Listening Active listening is more than hearing; it's about truly immersing yourself in the melody of another's words. Just as a musician listens intently to each note, a salesperson listens attentively to every nuance of a client's message. Active listening requires being present, absorbing not just words, but emotions, motivations, and unspoken needs. It's the rhythm of empathy that underscores understanding.

Creating Rhythms of Rapport is the melody that turns strangers into allies. Just as a musician finds common chords, a salesperson seeks common ground to build rapport. It's about discovering shared experiences, interests, and values that harmonize your relationship. Rapport is the bridge that transforms transactions into connections, making clients feel understood and valued.

The Echoes of Validation is the echo that reverberates in meaningful conversations. Just as a refrain repeats, validation acknowledges the significance of another's thoughts. It's the acknowledgment that their words matter, and their perspective is valued. Validating a client's concerns or aspirations creates a resonant harmony, building trust and encouraging openness.

Mirroring: A Melodic Technique Mirroring is the technique of reflecting a client's communication style. Just as a skilled musician adapts to the mood of a song, a salesperson mirrors a client's pace, tone, and style of communication. This subtle harmony creates a sense of familiarity, enhancing comfort and deepening connection.

Conclusion: A Duet of Connection Active listening and building rapport are the duet that transforms sales interactions into meaningful dialogues. They're the rhythm and melody that intertwine, creating harmonious connections with clients. When you listen actively and build rapport authentically, you're orchestrating a symphony of engagement where trust, understanding, and resonance reign. As a sales professional, you have the power to compose conversations that linger in the hearts of your clients, creating harmonies of lasting connection.

Nonverbal Communication: The Dance of Influence

In the grand orchestra of sales, words are only one instrument. The rest of the melody is composed through the artful dance of nonverbal communication and body language. Picture yourself leading a graceful dance that speaks volumes even without a single word – that's the power of nonverbal communication.

The Language of Gestures Think of your body as a palette of expressive gestures. A warm smile can be a welcoming embrace, while a confident posture exudes self-assuredness. Just like a conductor uses hand gestures to guide the orchestra, you can employ purposeful movements to direct the flow of a sales conversation.

Mirroring: The Dance of Connection Imagine a waltz where partners mirror each other's steps. In sales, mirroring is your dance of connection. Subtly matching your prospect's body language creates a harmonious rapport. When they lean in, you lean in; when they nod, you nod. This dance synchronizes your energies, forging a deeper bond.

Eye Contact: The Gaze of Confidence Imagine your eyes as spotlights that illuminate your message. Steady eye contact communicates confidence and sincerity. It's like looking directly at your audience while delivering a powerful solo. Your eyes draw them in, helping them trust and believe in the narrative you're weaving.

Space and Proximity: The Comforting Embrace Imagine the physical space between you and your prospect as a delicate dance floor. Respect personal space; don't invade it like a clumsy dancer. Striking the right balance of proximity creates a sense of intimacy without discomfort, just like a well-choreographed duet.

Gestures and Cues: The Subtle Harmony Imagine your gestures as notes, punctuating your conversation. Subtle hand movements emphasize key points, like a musician adding embellishments to a melody. Use open palms to convey openness and closed fists to express determination. Your movements are the visual melody of your words.

Conclusion: Your Dance of Influence In the mesmerizing realm of sales, nonverbal communication and body language are your dance of influence. You orchestrate trust with a warm smile, waltz into rapport through mirroring, and deliver solos of confidence with unwavering eye contact. Your movements are the rhythm, and your gestures are the harmonies that guide your sales symphony. Master this dance, and you'll find yourself not only communicating but connecting on a level that words alone can't reach. So, step onto the stage of nonverbal communication, and let your dance of influence leave an indelible mark in the hearts of your prospects.

Chapter 4. The Spark of Discovery: Prospecting and Lead Generation

Imagine a treasure hunt where every step leads to a potential gem waiting to be unearthed. Welcome to the world of prospecting and lead generation, where the thrill of discovery fuels the fire of success. In this chapter, we embark on a journey to uncover hidden opportunities and learn how to turn prospects into valued leads.

The Essence of Prospecting is the compass guiding you to uncharted territories. Just as a treasure hunter identifies promising locations, a salesperson seeks out potential clients. It's about recognizing where your products or services align with needs, like discovering a buried treasure that perfectly fits your map.

Navigating the Landscape of Leads are the stars that light up your sales sky. Just as constellations guide sailors, leads guide salespeople toward potential customers. Leads come in various forms: cold, warm, and hot, each representing a different degree of readiness. Nurturing leads is like tending to stars, watching them twinkle with potential.

Fishing in the Right Pond: Targeting is the art of precision in prospecting. Imagine a fisherman casting a line in a specific spot known for abundant catch. In sales, targeting is identifying the ideal demographics, industries, or niches that match your offerings. It's about fishing in the pond most likely to yield the kind of fish you're seeking.

Creating Lures: Crafting Irresistible Offers Just as a fisherman selects the perfect bait, a salesperson creates alluring offers. Craft your message to resonate with your prospects' pain points and aspirations. Like a bait that catches the attention of a fish, your offer should be impossible for prospects to ignore.

The Dance of Follow-Up is the rhythm that keeps the prospecting dance alive. Imagine a partner in a graceful dance; follow-up maintains the connection. It's about nurturing relationships, providing valuable information, and staying top-of-mind. Just as a partner's moves complement yours, follow-up aligns with the prospect's journey.

Referrals: The Ripple Effect Referrals are the ripples that spread your influence. Imagine throwing a pebble in a pond and watching the ripples expand. Referrals work similarly; a satisfied client's recommendation creates waves of potential leads. It's the magic of word-of-mouth that amplifies your reach.

Conclusion: The Discovery Continues Prospecting and lead generation are the heartbeats of your sales journey, where every interaction is a step toward uncovering opportunities. Like an explorer charting new territories, you have the tools to identify potential gems and nurture them into valuable leads. With prospecting, every dial, email, or meeting is a chance to reveal a hidden treasure, and with lead generation, each connection brings you closer to the stars of your sales universe. So, embrace the thrill of the hunt, for in the world of sales, every prospect is a potential adventure waiting to be discovered.

Identifying Target Audience: Unveiling Your Audience's Canvas

Imagine stepping into an art studio, ready to paint a masterpiece. Before your brush touches the canvas, you must first understand the colours, shapes, and emotions you want to convey. Similarly, in the realm of sales, identifying your target audience is like discovering the canvas upon which your sales strategies will unfold.

The Art of Precision: Defining Your Target Audience Much like an artist selects the perfect canvas size, you must define your target audience with precision. Who are they? What challenges do they face? What dreams do they harbour? These questions form the palette of knowledge that allows you to create a vivid portrayal of your ideal customer.

Creating Buyer Personas: The Characters of Your Story Just as characters bring life to a story, buyer personas breathe life into your sales efforts. Imagine crafting unique personas, each with its own personality, desires, and preferences. These personas become the protagonists in your sales narrative, guiding your strategies toward resonating with real individuals.

The Prism of Demographics and Psychographics Demographics are the basic hues that colour your canvas. Age, gender, location, and occupation form the backdrop against which your strategies will shine. But don't stop there. Delve deeper into psychographics – the emotions, values, and behaviours that create vibrant shades in your target audience's portrait.

Segmentation: Carving Your Canvas into Masterpieces Imagine an artist creating distinct sections on a canvas to bring out various elements of their vision. Similarly, segmentation is your tool to divide your target audience into meaningful groups. These segments allow you to tailor your strategies and messages with the precision of a brushstroke.

The Ideal Customer Profile: Painting the Perfect Picture Imagine stepping back from your canvas and admiring a completed masterpiece. Your ideal customer profile is that masterpiece, an intricate blend of demographics, psychographics, and segments. It's the embodiment of who you are striving to serve, a portrait that guides your every move in the sales arena.

Conclusion: The Art of Precision in Sales Just as an artist's canvas is a blank slate waiting to become a work of art, your target audience is a canvas for your sales success. By understanding the nuances of demographics, psychographics, and segmentation, you create a masterpiece of precision in your sales strategies. Your buyer personas are the vibrant characters that dance across this canvas, bringing your sales story to life. So, take up the brush of knowledge and paint your way to success, for in the realm of sales, identifying your target audience is the first stroke of brilliance in a masterpiece waiting to be unveiled.

Prospecting Methods: Crafting Your Sales Symphony

Just as a composer weaves various melodies to create a symphony, a salesperson fuses different prospecting methods to craft a harmonious path toward success. Each method is a note, contributing to the melody of your sales journey.

Cold Calling: Striking the First Chord Imagine a pianist's fingers confidently striking the keys to initiate a musical piece. Cold calling, akin to that initial chord, is your bold entrance into the prospect's world. With a well-prepared script and a confident tone, you introduce yourself and your offering, hoping to strike a chord of interest.

Networking: The Ensemble of Connections Imagine a group of musicians working together to create a beautiful ensemble. Networking, much like that harmonious collaboration, involves building connections. Attend events, engage on social platforms, and form relationships that resonate. The beauty lies in the diverse tunes these connections bring to your sales composition.

Referrals: The Melodic Echoes of Trust Imagine a sweet melody echoing in a vast concert hall. Referrals are like those echoes, spreading the resonance of trust. A satisfied customer's recommendation resonates deeply, carrying the harmony of their endorsement. Embrace the power of referrals, as they introduce potential prospects to the rhythm of your offering.

Social Media: The Digital Symphony Imagine a symphony played through digital platforms, each note a social media post. Social media, like a digital orchestra, allows you to reach a wider audience. Share engaging content, participate in discussions, and compose a digital symphony that resonates with your target audience.

Content Marketing: Crafting Harmonious Narratives Imagine a composer weaving a narrative through music. Content marketing, a similar art, involves crafting narratives that resonate with your audience. Through blog posts, videos, and infographics, you tell stories that captivate, educate, and guide prospects toward your offerings.

Conclusion: The Symphony of Prospecting In the realm of sales, prospecting methods are the notes that compose your symphony of success. Cold calling strikes the first chord of engagement, networking forms the ensemble of connections, and referrals echo the trust you've built. Social media and content marketing join in to create a harmonious narrative that resonates with your audience. Just as a symphony's beauty lies in its arrangement of diverse melodies, your prospecting methods harmonize to create a melody of engagement, connection, and conversion. So, conduct your sales symphony with skill and artistry, and watch as the notes of prospecting methods blend into a crescendo of successful sales melodies.

Harnessing Technology: The Digital Key to Lead Generation

In the dynamic world of sales, technology isn't just a tool; it's a mighty ally that opens doors to vast landscapes of opportunity. Welcome to the age where algorithms and innovation merge to transform the way we generate leads and unlock unprecedented growth.

Digital Footprints: Tracing Paths to Prospects Imagine the digital realm as a treasure map, with each click and interaction leaving a trace. Technology lets you follow these digital footprints, uncovering potential leads with precision. From social media platforms to search engines, every click is a potential clue leading you to a goldmine of prospects.

CRM Magic: Organizing Leads with Finesse Picture a magical tome that keeps track of every interaction you've ever had. That's what a Customer Relationship Management (CRM) system is for salespeople. It's your enchanted book of contacts, conversations, and conversions. It sorts, categorizes, and recalls information so you can approach leads with tailored finesse.

Automated Outreach: The Messenger of the Digital Age Imagine sending personalized messages to dozens of leads simultaneously, each message tailored to the recipient's interests. With technology, this isn't a fantasy; it's automated outreach. Email campaigns, social media automations, and chatbots are your digital messengers, delivering your pitch with efficiency and accuracy.

Analytics Alchemy: Turning Data into Gold Imagine a crystal ball that reveals the future – that's what analytics can be for lead generation. Technology transforms data into insights, unveiling trends, preferences, and patterns. With these insights, you can predict and strategize, casting spells of relevance that resonate with your target audience.

Social Media Sorcery: Casting a Wider Net Imagine a global gathering where everyone shares their interests openly – that's social media. Platforms like Facebook, LinkedIn, and Twitter are modern-day marketplaces. By crafting magnetic content, engaging in conversations, and targeting specific demographics, you cast a spell of visibility, drawing leads like moths to a flame.

SEO Enchantment: Making Your Presence Known Imagine a magical incantation that makes you appear whenever someone seeks your expertise – that's Search Engine Optimization (SEO). By sprinkling keywords into your online content, you ensure that when leads search for solutions, you're the wizard they find, ready to guide them on their journey.

Conclusion: Weaving the Digital Tapestry of Leads In the tapestry of lead generation, technology is the warp and weft that holds it all together. It helps you follow the digital trails of prospects, organize them with the precision of a maestro, and automate outreach with the efficiency of clockwork. It empowers you to turn data into golden insights and cast spells of visibility across social media realms. With technology as your trusted ally, you're not just generating leads; you're conjuring connections and crafting a legacy of growth. So, embrace this digital magic, for in this age, your success story is written not just in ink, but in lines of code and algorithms that propel you forward in the realm of sales.

5. Crafting Compelling Sales Presentations: Your Path to Captivation

Step onto the stage of sales presentations, where your words and visuals come together in a symphony of persuasion. In this realm, you're not just sharing information; you're weaving stories that captivate hearts and minds. Welcome to the art of creating sales presentations that leave an indelible mark.

Storytelling Sorcery: The Heartbeat of Engagement Imagine being around a campfire, listening to a mesmerizing tale. That's the magic of storytelling, and it's your secret weapon in creating compelling presentations. Weave narratives that resonate with your audience's desires, fears, and aspirations, drawing them into a world where your product or service is the hero they've been waiting for.

Visual Enchantment: The Power of Imagery Imagine a canvas that transforms ideas into visual masterpieces – that's the role of visuals in your presentation. Infographics, images, and videos breathe life into your words, making complex concepts simple to understand and impossible to forget. The right visual can be the key that unlocks comprehension and connection.

Simplicity Spell: Speak Their Language Imagine speaking a language that everyone understands – that's simplicity. Your audience is diverse, so ditch the jargon and convey your message with crystal clarity. When your presentation is a breeze to comprehend, your listeners feel like you're speaking directly to them, forging a connection that lingers.

Benefit Elixir: Showcasing Value Imagine a fountain that pours forth the benefits your product offers – that's what your presentation should be. Highlight the value your audience gains by showing them how your solution transforms their lives. Each benefit you present is like a sip of elixir, rejuvenating their desire to explore further.

Interactive Magic: Involve and Conquer Imagine a magic wand that lets your audience participate – that's interactivity. Engage your listeners by asking questions, conducting polls, or encouraging them to share their experiences. When they actively participate, they're not just observers; they're co-creators of the journey you're taking them on.

Audience Connection: Meeting Them Where They Are Imagine being the guide who knows every path – that's the magic of audience-centred presentations. Tailor your content to their interests, challenges, and aspirations. By demonstrating that you understand their world, you form a connection that transforms strangers into allies.

Call to Action Charm: Sealing the Deal Imagine a spell that compels action – that's your call to action (CTA). Conclude your presentation by clearly and compellingly inviting your audience to take the next step. Whether it's making a purchase, booking a demo, or signing up for updates, your CTA is the pivotal moment when interest transforms into action.

Conclusion: You're the Enchanter of Minds In the realm of sales presentations, you're not just a speaker; you're a sorcerer of influence. You wield the magic of storytelling, weave visuals that resonate, and simplify complex ideas into pure understanding. With benefits as your elixir and interactivity as your wand, you transport your audience into a realm where they feel understood and valued. As you cast your call-to-action charm, you're not just presenting; you're orchestrating a journey towards partnership. Embrace this role with confidence, for you're not just creating compelling presentations; you're leaving a trail of enchanted minds in your wake.

Unleash Your Creative Sales Pitch: The Art of Unforgettable Persuasion

Welcome to the realm where creativity meets sales, where your pitch isn't just a presentation—it's an unforgettable experience. In this world of imagination and ingenuity, your pitch becomes a captivating story that leads your audience to say, "Yes, this is what I've been waiting for!"

Start with a Bang: The Opening Act Imagine the spotlight on a grand stage – that's your opening line. Capture attention from the very beginning with a compelling hook that sparks curiosity and ignites interest. Whether it's a thought-provoking question or a surprising fact, this is the moment where you draw them in, like a magician revealing their first trick.

Paint a Vivid Picture: The Story Unfolds Imagine being a master storyteller, weaving an intricate tapestry – that's your role in the creative pitch. Take your audience on a journey with your words, painting a vivid picture of the problem they face and the solution you're offering. Immerse them in a narrative that resonates, making them feel like the hero of their own story.

Inject Playfulness: The Magic of Metaphors Imagine sprinkling enchanting metaphors like fairy dust – that's how you infuse playfulness into your pitch. Compare your product to something unexpected, turning the mundane into the magical. Metaphors not only simplify complex ideas but also create a sense of wonder that lingers long after your pitch is over.

Leverage Visuals: The Artistry of Slides Imagine your slides as a canvas for your ideas – that's where visual creativity shines. Design slides that are visually appealing, using images, infographics, and minimal text to convey messages at a glance. Each slide should be a work of art that enhances the emotional impact of your pitch.

Interactive Brilliance: Engaging Participation Imagine your pitch as a lively conversation – that's the power of interactivity. Involve your audience with questions, polls, or even mini activities that encourage participation. By engaging them directly, you're not just presenting; you're building a connection that keeps them invested.

Tailored Enchantment: Speak Their Language Imagine having a key to unlock every door – that's the magic of tailoring your pitch. Customize your pitch to resonate with your audience's needs, challenges, and aspirations. Show them that you've done your homework and understand their world, creating a connection that's impossible to resist.

Address Objections with Finesse: The Plot Twist Imagine turning obstacles into steppingstones – that's how you handle objections. Anticipate concerns your audience might have and address them seamlessly within your pitch. This demonstrates your expertise and shows that you're one step ahead, building trust and credibility.

Unveil the Grand Finale: The Call to Action Imagine a crescendo that leaves the audience in awe – that's your call to action (CTA). Conclude your pitch by leading them to the next step, whether it's a trial, a demonstration, or a purchase. Craft a CTA that's not just a command but an invitation to continue this thrilling journey.

Conclusion: You're the Architect of Inspiration In the realm of creative sales pitching, you're not just presenting; you're crafting a masterpiece of persuasion. Your opening is the spotlight that shines on curiosity, your story is the tapestry of connection, and your metaphors are the enchanting spells that captivate. Visuals transform your pitch into a canvas of emotion, while interactivity turns listeners into participants. With tailored charm and objection-handling finesse, you create an experience that resonates deeply. And as you orchestrate the grand finale—the call to action—you're not just ending; you're extending an invitation to embark on a transformative journey. Embrace this role with flair, for you're not just delivering a pitch; you're crafting a tale of irresistible allure and boundless possibility.

Unleash the Power of Engaging Visuals and Storytelling: Elevating Your Sales Game

Welcome to the realm where visuals and storytelling converge, where your sales pitch isn't just a presentation—it's an immersive journey. In this world of captivating narratives and striking visuals, your pitch becomes an experience that leaves an indelible mark on your audience.

The Art of Visuals: Painting with Imagination Imagine your visuals as strokes of a painter's brush—each one contributing to the masterpiece. Visual elements like images, infographics, and videos have the power to evoke emotions, simplify complex ideas, and create lasting memories. Your visuals should be more than just decoration; they should be integral to the story you're telling.

Crafting a Visual Narrative: From Chaos to Clarity Imagine your visuals as puzzle pieces—fitting together to reveal the bigger picture. Your sales pitch should unfold like a story, with each visual element seamlessly guiding your audience from one point to the next. Whether it's a flowchart illustrating a process or a before-and-after comparison, your visuals should clarify, not confuse.

Weaving the Story: From Words to Emotions Imagine being a master weaver, intertwining threads to create a tapestry of emotions. Storytelling is the backbone of engagement, and every successful sales pitch is a narrative that resonates. Begin with a relatable protagonist (your customer), set the stage with their challenges, and introduce your product as the transformative solution. Paint vivid mental images that evoke empathy and create a sense of urgency.

Tapping into Emotion: The Heart of Connection Imagine your audience not just listening but feeling—the emotion is your gateway. Emotions are the bridge between your story and your audience's experiences. Whether it's using anecdotes, testimonials, or even a well-timed pause, infuse your narrative with emotional triggers that make your message relatable and impactful.

Fostering Engagement: The Interactive Experience Imagine your pitch as a dialogue, not a monologue—engagement is the key. Use interactive elements to involve your audience, such as asking questions, conducting polls, or incorporating real-time examples. Interaction transforms passive listeners into active participants, ensuring that they remain engaged throughout the journey.

Visual Consistency: A Symphony of Design Imagine your visuals as a harmonious ensemble—consistent in style and tone. Whether it's colour schemes, font choices, or visual motifs, maintaining visual consistency enhances brand recognition and creates a professional impression. A cohesive visual identity instils trust and credibility.

The Power of Analogies: Bridging Understanding Imagine your pitch as a bridge, connecting the unknown to the known—this is the magic of analogies. Analogies simplify complex concepts by comparing them to something familiar. Whether it's likening your product's benefits to a superhero's powers or explaining a technical process using a cooking metaphor, analogies illuminate the path of comprehension.

Conclusion: Crafting the Unforgettable Journey In the realm of engaging visuals and storytelling, you're not just delivering information; you're sculpting an experience. Your visuals are brushstrokes that paint emotions, while your story is the tapestry that weaves empathy and urgency. Embrace emotions, ignite interaction, and foster consistency to create a symphony of engagement. Through analogies, you build bridges of understanding that span gaps in comprehension. And as your pitch concludes, your audience won't just remember what you said; they'll remember how you made them feel. Embrace the role of visual storyteller with gusto, for you're not just pitching; you're inviting your audience on a transformative journey they'll never forget.

Addressing Customer Needs and Pain Points: The Compass to Connection

Welcome to the compass of customer-centric sales, where understanding needs and alleviating pain points isn't a task—it's a guiding principle. In this realm of empathy and solutions, your mission is to illuminate the path towards satisfaction.

Embrace Empathetic Inquiry: The Art of Listening Beyond Words Imagine yourself as a detective, unearthing hidden clues—empathetic inquiry is your magnifying glass. Listen not just to the words, but to the emotions behind them. Ask open-ended questions that invite customers to share their challenges, desires, and aspirations. Understand their world, and you'll earn their trust.

Identify the Pain Points: Where Problems Seek Solutions Imagine pain points as locked doors—your task is to find the right key. Pain points are the challenges customers face, the hurdles they need to overcome. Through conversations and research, pinpoint these obstacles and acknowledge them. Show customers that you understand their struggles.

Map the Journey: Walking in Their Shoes Imagine yourself in your customer's shoes, navigating their path—this is the journey map. Trace their experience from the beginning to the end. Where do they encounter difficulties? What could be smoother? Use this map to identify critical touchpoints where your solution can make a difference.

Crafting Tailored Solutions: The Elixir of Relief Imagine your solution as a balm that soothes discomfort—tailoring is the key. Once you've uncovered pain points, create solutions that directly address them. This is where your product or service becomes a remedy. Show customers that not only do you understand their problems, but you also have the antidote.

Benefits that Shine: Illuminating Transformation Imagine benefits as beacons of light in the darkness—each one guiding towards a better future. Once you've identified pain points and tailored solutions, highlight the benefits. Showcase the positive transformation your solution offers. Paint a vivid picture of how their life could be enhanced by choosing your offering.

Bridge with Value: From Solution to Impact Imagine your solution as a bridge that connects pain to relief—value is your bridge's foundation. Clearly communicate the value your solution brings. Demonstrate how it directly addresses their pain points and improves their situation. Use real-world examples or case studies to illustrate the impact.

Empower with Knowledge: Guiding Informed Decisions Imagine yourself as a lantern bearer, illuminating the path of choice—knowledge is your lantern. Equip customers with information to make informed decisions. Explain how your solution aligns with their needs and the positive changes it can bring. Transparency fosters trust.

Conclusion: A Symphony of Solutions and Empathy In the realm of addressing customer needs and pain points, you're not just selling a product—you're offering a remedy. Through empathetic inquiry, you uncover the hidden threads of pain. By crafting tailored solutions, you mend those threads with benefits that shine. The bridge of value guides customers towards transformation, and your lantern of knowledge ensures they make informed choices. In this symphony of solutions and empathy, you don't just solve problems; you cultivate connections built on understanding and relief. Embrace the role of a problem solver with compassion, for you're not just addressing pain points; you're kindling the flames of trust and transformation.

Chapter 6. Negotiation and Closing Techniques: The Art of Crafting Win-Win Agreements

Welcome to the realm where deals are sealed, and mutual satisfaction is the crown jewel. In this chapter, we dive deep into the world of negotiation and closing techniques—a domain where strategies, finesse, and communication dance together to orchestrate successful outcomes.

Imagine negotiation as a captivating dance—a rhythm of exchange, where both parties move toward a harmonious resolution. Your role as a salesperson is not just to secure a deal but to create a win-win scenario where everyone leaves the floor with a sense of accomplishment.

In this chapter, we will unravel the secrets of effective negotiation and closing techniques. We'll explore the psychology behind successful negotiations, the art of handling objections, and the power of persuasive communication. By the end, you'll be equipped with the tools to guide potential clients from hesitation to agreement, transforming mere interest into a solid commitment.

So, put on your negotiation shoes, and let's step into the realm where opportunities are seized, objections are overcome, and agreements are forged. Whether you're a seasoned sales professional or embarking on your journey, this chapter will illuminate the path to mastering negotiation and achieving the coveted art of closing deals.

Understanding Negotiation Dynamics: Deciphering the Dance of Deals

Negotiation is the heart of sales—the art of reaching agreements that satisfy both parties' needs and desires. It's a dance where skilful moves, strategic thinking, and effective communication are essential to guide the process toward a successful outcome. In this chapter, we'll delve into the intricate world of negotiation dynamics, equipping you with the knowledge and insights to navigate this artful dance with finesse.

The Dance Begins: Unveiling Negotiation Dynamics

Picture yourself stepping onto the negotiation floor. It's not just a matter of presenting figures and facts; it's a psychological interplay of motives, emotions, and perceptions. Understanding negotiation dynamics requires a blend of empathy, strategy, and adaptability.

Building Blocks of Negotiation Dynamics

Goals and Interests: At the heart of every negotiation lie the goals and interests of both parties. As a skilled negotiator, your role is to uncover these hidden gems. Are you negotiating for a lower price, faster delivery, or additional services? Equally important, what are the client's aspirations and needs? By aligning these factors, you pave the way for a mutually beneficial agreement.

Power Dynamics: Negotiations often involve varying levels of power between parties. It could be influenced by factors like industry expertise, market conditions, or time constraints. Understanding power dynamics helps you approach negotiations with sensitivity and adapt your strategy accordingly.

Communication: Effective negotiation hinges on clear and persuasive communication. Active listening, concise articulation, and the ability to read between the lines are your allies. Remember, it's not just about what is said, but also about what isn't.

Objections and Solutions: Objections are the natural companions of negotiations. They are not roadblocks but opportunities to address concerns. Learn to dissect objections, understand their roots, and craft solutions that showcase how your offering meets the client's needs.

Flexibility and Adaptability: In the dance of negotiation, rigid moves rarely succeed. Be prepared to adapt your approach based on the evolving dynamics of the conversation. Flexibility signals your commitment to finding common ground.

Mastering the Dance: Key Negotiation Strategies

Win-Win Mindset: Negotiation isn't a zero-sum game; it's about creating value for both sides. Embrace the win-win mindset, seeking solutions that address both parties' interests.

Anchoring and Framing: The way you present information can influence perceptions. Anchoring involves starting with an extreme offer and then gradually moving toward a reasonable middle ground. Framing involves presenting options in a way that highlights their benefits.

Exploring Options: Expand the playing field by exploring multiple options. Creativity can lead to innovative solutions that were initially unseen.

Building Rapport: Establishing a positive and collaborative atmosphere can significantly impact negotiations. Building rapport fosters trust and open communication.

Emotional Intelligence: Emotions can sway negotiations. Being attuned to the emotional undercurrents allows you to respond with empathy and maintain a productive dialogue.

The Grand Finale: Reaching Agreement

The culmination of negotiation is the agreement—an intricate balance of compromise and alignment. The successful negotiator understands that closing a deal doesn't mean sacrificing value but rather optimizing outcomes.

In this chapter, you'll gain the tools to decipher negotiation dynamics, apply strategic manoeuvres, and forge agreements that satisfy both parties. Just like any dance, practice refines your skills. Embrace negotiation as an art form, an opportunity to create value, and a testament to your prowess as a sales professional. With every negotiation, you embark on a unique journey, transforming challenges into triumphs, and agreements into lasting partnerships. So, let's step into the rhythm of negotiation dynamics and master the dance of deals.

Overcoming Objections and Handling Rejections: Turning Challenges into Opportunities

In the exhilarating world of sales, objections and rejections are like crossroads that test your mettle. Far from being roadblocks, they are opportunities to showcase your expertise, resilience, and problem-solving prowess. In this chapter, we'll delve into the art of overcoming objections and handling rejections with finesse, transforming challenges into steppingstones toward success.

Objections: The Unveiling of Concerns

Objections are the signs of an engaged prospect—a cue that they're invested enough to raise concerns. Far from being disheartening, objections are openings to provide clarity and demonstrate your commitment to understanding their needs.

Mastering the Objection Dance

Active Listening: When an objection surfaces, listen attentively. Behind every objection lies a need or a misunderstanding. By truly understanding their concern, you can tailor your response effectively.

Empathy: Acknowledge the prospect's perspective. Empathy bridges gaps, fostering trust and showing that you value their point of view.

Address Concerns Head-On: Approach objections as puzzles waiting to be solved. Provide clear, concise, and relevant information that assuages their concerns and highlights the value your product or service offers.

Highlight Solutions: Turn objections into opportunities to showcase the solutions your offering provides. Paint a vivid picture of how your product addresses their pain points.

Stories and Examples: Human beings relate to stories. Share success stories or case studies where your solution resolved similar concerns. It's a powerful way to demonstrate real-world impact.

Handling Rejections: A Pivot Point

Rejections are not failures; they're invitations to grow. Handling rejections with grace and professionalism can actually enhance your reputation in the eyes of prospects.

Rejection as Feedback

De-Personalize Rejections: Remember, a rejection isn't a personal critique. It's often a mismatch between the prospect's needs and your solution. Keep your confidence intact.

Seek Feedback: After a rejection, politely ask for feedback. This insight can provide invaluable guidance for improvement.

The Silver Lining: Turning Rejections into Opportunities

Persistence Pays: Sometimes a "no" today can turn into a "yes" tomorrow. Stay on your prospect's radar with relevant content and respectful follow-ups.

Professionalism: How you handle rejection can leave a lasting impression. A courteous and professional response can lead to referrals or even reconsideration.

Continuous Improvement: Each rejection is a chance to refine your approach. Analyse what worked and what didn't and use this insight to refine your pitch.

The Art of Overcoming: Crafting Responses

Preparation is Key: Anticipate objections and craft thoughtful responses in advance. This preparation demonstrates your expertise and confidence.

Customize Responses: Tailor your responses to the specific concerns of each prospect. Generic replies can come across as insincere.

Bridge to Benefits: Turn objections into a springboard to highlight benefits. Demonstrate how your solution outweighs their concerns.

The Victory of Conversion: Overcoming and Winning

In the dance of objections and rejections, your role is that of a problem solver and educator. Every objection presents an opportunity to deepen your prospect's understanding and lead them closer to a decision.

As you navigate the waters of objections and gracefully handle rejections, you demonstrate resilience and adaptability. Each challenge you overcome adds a brushstroke to the masterpiece of your sales journey. With each objection addressed, you inch closer to building trust, fostering partnerships, and achieving your sales goals. Embrace objections and rejections not as deterrents, but as pathways to growth and triumph. Step forth into the realm of overcoming, ready to turn challenges into opportunities and objections into victories.

Common Objections

1. Price Objection: Objection: "Your product is too expensive." Response: "I understand that pricing is an important consideration. Let me share with you the long-term benefits and return on investment our product offers. It can help increase your efficiency and save costs in the long run, making it a worthwhile investment."

2. Product Fit Objection: Objection: "I'm not sure if your product is the right fit for our needs." Response: "I appreciate your concern. Let's go over your specific needs in detail. Our product is highly customizable, and I'm confident we can tailor it to perfectly meet your requirements."

3. Competitor Comparison Objection: Objection: "I've seen a similar product from your competitor." Response: "It's essential to compare offerings before making a decision. Let me highlight the unique features and advantages our product has over our competitors. Additionally, we provide excellent customer support and a proven track record of customer satisfaction."

4. Timing Objection: Objection: "We're not ready to make a decision right now." Response: "I understand that timing is crucial for your decision-making process. Can we schedule a follow-up call to discuss your timeline further? This way, we can ensure we align with your preferred schedule."

5. Authority Objection: Objection: "I need to consult with my boss before making a decision." Response: "I completely understand the need to involve your boss in the decision. To assist with the conversation, I can provide additional materials and case studies that demonstrate the value our product has brought to other companies."

6. Need for Additional Features Objection: Objection: "Your product doesn't have all the features we need." Response: "Thank you for sharing your requirements. We value feedback from our customers, and I'll pass on your request for additional features to our product development team. In

the meantime, I can show you how our current features can still address many of your needs."

7. Lack of Trust Objection: Objection: "I'm not sure if I can trust your company." Response: "Building trust is essential for us too. Let me share some testimonials and success stories from our satisfied customers. Additionally, we have been in business for [number of years], and our team is dedicated to providing exceptional service."

8. Risk Aversion Objection: Objection: "I'm hesitant to try something new." Response: "It's natural to be cautious when trying something new. To ease your concerns, we offer a trial period so you can experience the benefits firsthand. We also have a money-back guarantee if you're not satisfied with the results."

9. Budget Constraint Objection: Objection: "Your product is beyond our budget." Response: "I understand budget limitations, and we can work together to find a solution that fits your budget. Let's explore which features are most crucial for your needs and see if we can customize a package that aligns with your financial goals."

10. Previous Negative Experience Objection: Objection: "We had a bad experience with a similar product in the past." Response: "I'm sorry to hear about your past experience. Our company takes customer satisfaction seriously, and we've implemented changes to improve our product and service. Let me share how we've addressed the issues to ensure a positive experience with us."

Remember, the key to overcoming objections is to actively listen, acknowledge the prospect's concerns, and provide relevant information to address their doubts. Tailor your responses to each prospect's unique situation and demonstrate empathy to build trust and rapport. By addressing objections effectively, you can increase the likelihood of closing the sale and fostering long-lasting customer relationships.

Strategies for Effective Closing: Mastering the Art of Sealing the Deal

In this section, we'll explore the crucial strategies and techniques that can turn a promising interaction into a successful conversion. Mastering the art of closing is like the grand finale of a performance – it requires finesse, timing, and a deep understanding of your customer's needs.

Section 1: The Art of Timing and Confidence

1.1 Understanding the Buying Signals Identifying subtle buying signals from your prospect is key. Watch for positive body language, enthusiastic responses, and questions about contract terms or next steps. These cues indicate a potential readiness to close.

1.2 The Power of Confidence in yourself and your product is contagious. When you exude assurance and enthusiasm, it reassures your prospect that they're making the right choice. Confidence helps build trust and encourages the prospect to follow your lead.

Section 2: The Trial Close Approach

2.1 Testing the Waters Before going in for the final close, consider a trial close. Ask questions like, "If we can address all your concerns, are you ready to move forward?" This gauges the prospect's current mindset and allows you to overcome any remaining objections.

2.2 Tailoring Your Pitch Based on the trial close response, fine-tune your pitch for the final close. Address objections that may have surfaced and emphasize the benefits that align with the prospect's needs.

Section 3: Assumptive Close Techniques

3.1 Paint the Picture Use assumptive language that implies the deal is already closed. For instance, say, "When we get started..." rather than "If you decide to proceed..." This technique subtly guides the prospect towards envisioning the partnership.

3.2 The Choice of Alternatives Present the prospect with a choice between two favourable options. This technique offers control while nudging them towards a positive decision. For example, "Would you prefer implementation in June or July?"

Section 4: Creating a Sense of Urgency

4.1 Limited-Time Offers Introduce limited-time offers or promotions that encourage prompt action. Time-sensitive incentives can create a sense of urgency, motivating the prospect to make a decision sooner rather than later.

4.2 Highlighting Benefits of Timely Action Explain the benefits the prospect will experience by acting promptly. Whether it's gaining a competitive edge, maximizing a seasonal opportunity, or enjoying immediate savings, emphasizing these advantages can trigger the desire to close quickly.

Section 5: Overcoming Final Objections

5.1 Last-Minute Objections Address any remaining objections that might arise during the closing phase. Reiterate the value proposition, provide additional evidence, or clarify any misconceptions to alleviate concerns.

Section 6: The Assured Follow-Up

6.1 Outlining the Next Steps After the deal is closed, clearly outline the next steps and the timeline for implementation. This reassures the prospect that their decision will lead to a smooth transition and a positive experience.

Section 7: The Graceful Close

7.1 Respect the Decision Respect the prospect's decision, whether it's a "yes," a "no," or a request for more time. Show appreciation for their time and consideration and leave the door open for future interactions.

7.2 Express Gratitude Regardless of the outcome, express genuine gratitude for the opportunity to connect and discuss their needs. A positive and gracious attitude reflects professionalism and leaves a lasting impression.

Conclusion: The Art of Sealing the Deal

Mastering the art of closing is about creating a seamless transition from persuasive communication to successful conversion. By understanding buying signals, maintaining confidence, and employing various closing techniques, you can guide prospects towards the final decision. Remember that every interaction, objection, and connection contribute to your closing prowess. As you navigate the dynamic world of sales, approach each close with a sense of purpose and optimism, knowing that your strategic efforts can turn possibilities into prosperous partnerships.

Chapter 7: Building and Managing Customer Relationships: The Foundation of Long-Lasting Partnerships

Welcome to the chapter dedicated to the heart of successful sales: building and nurturing customer relationships. In this chapter, we'll explore the essential strategies and techniques that transform one-time transactions into enduring partnerships. Just as a skilled gardener tends to their plants, nurturing customer relationships requires care, attention, and a deep commitment to growth.

Section 1: The Power of Customer Relationships

1.1 Understanding the Value of Relationships In the world of sales, relationships are the bedrock of sustainable success. Strong customer relationships lead to repeat business, referrals, and advocates who sing your praises to others.

1.2 The Ripple Effect Positive relationships with your customers have a ripple effect that extends beyond just that individual interaction. Satisfied clients become your brand ambassadors, sharing their positive experiences with their networks.

Section 2: The Art of Relationship Building

2.1 Personalized Communication Treat every customer as an individual with unique needs. Personalize your communication and show genuine interest in their concerns, challenges, and goals.

2.2 Empathy and Understanding Put yourself in your customer's shoes. Understand their pain points and aspirations. Empathy allows you to tailor your approach and offer solutions that truly resonate.

Section 3: Consistent Engagement and Follow-Up

3.1 Timely Follow-Ups After a sale, maintain regular follow-up to ensure the customer's satisfaction. A simple check-in or a "how are things going?" can go a long way in solidifying the relationship.

3.2 Providing Value Continue to offer value beyond the initial sale. Share relevant content, industry insights, and tips that help your customers succeed in their endeavours.

Section 4: Active Listening and Feedback Loop

4.1 Listening to Understand Active listening involves more than just hearing words; it's about truly understanding what your customers are saying. Listen intently to their feedback, concerns, and ideas.

4.2 Addressing Concerns When issues arise, address them promptly and proactively. Use negative feedback as an opportunity to demonstrate your commitment to customer satisfaction.

Section 5: Going Above and Beyond

5.1 Surprise and Delight Small gestures can make a big impact. Sending a thank-you note, offering exclusive perks, or remembering a customer's birthday can create a memorable experience.

Section 6: Leveraging Technology for Relationship Management

6.1 Customer Relationship Management (CRM) Systems Utilize CRM systems to keep track of customer interactions, preferences, and history. This data empowers you to offer tailored solutions and personalized service.

Section 7: The Art of Handling Difficult Situations

7.1 Turning Challenges into Opportunities Difficult situations can be a chance to showcase your dedication to customer satisfaction. Resolve issues promptly, go the extra mile, and turn negatives into positives.

Section 8: Celebrating Milestones

8.1 Acknowledging Achievements Celebrate your customers' milestones – whether it's an anniversary, a major achievement, or a milestone in their business. Recognize their successes and reinforce your support.

Section 9: Long-Term Relationship Development

9.1 Growing with Your Customers As your customers' needs evolve, adapt your solutions to meet them. Position yourself as a partner who is invested in their growth and success.

Conclusion: Nurturing Partnerships for Lifelong Success

Building and managing customer relationships is a journey, not a destination. By personalizing your communication, providing consistent value, and showing genuine care, you transform each transaction into a steppingstone toward a lasting partnership. Approach your customer relationships with an open heart, a commitment to understanding, and a genuine desire to contribute to their success. As you navigate the landscape of sales, remember that the bonds you cultivate today can blossom into fruitful partnerships that stand the test of time.

The Heart of Success: The Importance of Relationship-Building in Sales

In the vibrant tapestry of the sales world, one thread shines brighter than the rest – the art of relationship-building. Imagine sales not as transactions, but as the nurturing of connections that flourish over time. These connections aren't just bridges to deals; they are the foundation upon which success is built.

Creating the Human Connection

At the heart of relationship-building lies the power of human connection. We're not just selling products or services; we're touching lives, solving problems, and fulfilling needs. This human connection transforms a salesperson from a mere vendor into a trusted partner, someone who understands the dreams and aspirations of their customers.

The Ripple Effect

One positive interaction can send ripples through the vast sea of potential customers. When you invest time in building relationships, you're not just gaining a single sale – you're unlocking a cascade of opportunities. Satisfied customers become the loudest advocates for your brand, sharing their positive experiences and influencing others to choose your solutions.

Trust: The Currency of Relationships

Trust, like sunlight, nourishes every aspect of a relationship. It's earned through transparent communication, consistent follow-ups, and a commitment to delivering value. When customers trust you, they're more likely to return, more willing to provide referrals, and more open to exploring new solutions you offer.

Longevity and Loyalty

Building relationships isn't about quick wins; it's about planting seeds for long-term growth. Customers who feel valued and understood are more likely to stay loyal over time. They become the bedrock of your success, forming a loyal customer base that's eager to engage in ongoing business.

Turning Challenges into Opportunities

Relationships shine most brightly in the face of adversity. When you encounter challenges, whether they're product-related issues or market shifts, strong relationships give you a cushion of goodwill. Customers who trust you are more patient and understanding, allowing you the chance to address problems and prove your commitment to their satisfaction.

A Journey of Mutual Growth

Think of relationship-building as a shared journey of growth. As you invest in understanding your customers' needs, challenges, and aspirations, you're not just pushing a sale; you're contributing to their success. The satisfaction of helping them achieve their goals becomes a wellspring of personal fulfilment, turning each transaction into a triumph of mutual accomplishment.

Conclusion: The Tapestry of Success

In the realm of sales, relationship-building isn't just a strategy; it's a way of life. It's a commitment to treating every interaction as an opportunity to create connections that resonate long after the deal is closed. By focusing on the human element, fostering trust, and nurturing loyalty, you weave a tapestry of success that's rich with enduring partnerships and the promise of a brighter future. So, step into the world of sales with open arms and a warm heart, ready to build relationships that illuminate the path to greatness.

Guiding the Journey: Customer Lifecycle Management

Imagine the world of sales as a grand voyage, and customers as intrepid travellers seeking solutions to their needs. This voyage doesn't end with a single purchase; it's a continuous cycle of interactions, growth, and mutual benefit. This journey is what we call the customer lifecycle, and managing it effectively is an art that fuels success in the sales realm.

The Lifecycle Unfolded

The customer lifecycle is a series of stages that a customer passes through, from the first spark of awareness to becoming a loyal advocate. It's not a linear path, but a dynamic process that requires nurturing, guidance, and adaptation. Understanding this cycle is like having a compass that helps you navigate the ever-changing tides of customer engagement.

Mapping the Stages

Awareness: The journey begins when a potential customer becomes aware of your offerings. This is your chance to make a compelling first impression that piques their interest.

Interest: As curiosity turns into interest, your role is to provide in-depth information, addressing their pain points and demonstrating how your solution can be the answer they seek.

Consideration: Here, customers are comparing options. Your task is to stand out by showcasing the unique value you bring to the table and building trust through transparent communication.

Decision: The decision-making stage is the culmination of your efforts. This is where the prospect becomes a customer. Clear communication and personalized incentives can tip the scales in your favour.

Purchase: Congratulations, you've made a sale! But remember, this is just one milestone in the journey.

Retention: Post-purchase, your focus shifts to maintaining engagement and ensuring customer satisfaction. A happy customer is more likely to return and refer others.

Advocacy: Delighted customers become your brand advocates, spreading positive word-of-mouth and contributing to your credibility.

The Magic of Lifecycle Management

The beauty of customer lifecycle management lies in the ability to tailor your approach to each stage. A one-size-fits-all strategy won't do; you need to provide the right content, support, and interactions at the right time. This level of personalization showcases your commitment to their journey, fostering stronger relationships.

A Symphony of Engagement

Picture the customer lifecycle as a symphony. Every stage has its own melody and tempo. Your role as a salesperson is to conduct this symphony, guiding customers seamlessly from one stage to the next. The harmony you create is what makes the journey memorable and satisfying, encouraging them to return for encore performances.

The Lifelong Connection

But the journey doesn't end here. The beauty of effective customer lifecycle management is that it doesn't stop after the sale; it circles back to the awareness stage. Satisfied customers can become repeat customers, initiating a new cycle of engagement. This cycle repeats, each time with the potential for deeper loyalty and more meaningful connections.

Conclusion: Navigating the Seas of Success

Customer lifecycle management is the lighthouse that guides your ship through the vast ocean of sales. By understanding the stages, personalizing your approach, and fostering enduring connections, you create a symphony of engagement that resonates long after the first interaction. So, set sail with purpose and enthusiasm, knowing that each customer interaction is a step towards creating a journey of mutual growth and lasting partnerships.

Crafting Unforgettable Experiences: Providing Exceptional Customer Service

In the realm of sales, the story doesn't conclude at the close of a deal. It's only the beginning of a relationship that can flourish into something truly exceptional. Welcome to the world of providing extraordinary customer service, where your commitment to creating memorable experiences sets the stage for lasting connections and boundless success.

The Heartbeat of Your Brand

Exceptional customer service isn't just a box to tick; it's the heartbeat of your brand. It's the promise you make and the commitment you keep. Think of each customer interaction as a chance to compose a melody of positivity and delight, leaving an indelible mark on their memory.

The Power of Personalization

In a world where transactions can feel cold and impersonal, your dedication to personalization stands as a beacon of warmth. Address customers by name, recall their preferences, and engage in conversations that show you genuinely care about their needs. This personal touch transforms a routine interaction into a cherished memory.

Listening: The Key to Understanding

Active listening is a superpower in the realm of customer service. By tuning in to your customers' needs, challenges, and feedback, you unlock a treasure trove of insights that guide your approach. This empathetic connection reassures them that they're valued, and their satisfaction is your priority.

Turning Problems into Opportunities

Mistakes happen; it's how you handle them that matters. A hiccup in the journey can be transformed into a moment of magic if you approach it with sincerity and dedication to finding solutions. When customers see your commitment to making things right, they're more likely to forgive and appreciate your efforts.

Going Above and Beyond

Exceptional service isn't about meeting expectations; it's about surpassing them. Imagine a guest at a five-star hotel receiving a personalized welcome note—this unexpected touch leaves a lasting impression. Similarly, anticipate your customers' needs and offer solutions they hadn't even considered.

The Ripple Effect

One extraordinary experience can set off a ripple effect. Satisfied customers become brand ambassadors, sharing their positive encounters with friends and family. This word-of-mouth marketing is priceless, reaching audiences you might never have reached through traditional means.

A Journey, not a Destination

Remember, exceptional customer service isn't a one-time effort; it's a continuous journey. Just as relationships evolve, so should your approach to serving your customers. Keep innovating, keep surprising, and keep evolving. Your commitment to excellence echoes through every touchpoint, creating a symphony of satisfaction.

Conclusion: Crafting Lasting Memories

Exceptional customer service is the art of crafting lasting memories. It's about more than just solving problems—it's about leaving an emotional imprint that lingers. As you navigate this realm, carry the torch of empathy, personalization, and genuine care. Every encounter is a chance to shine, and every delighted customer is a testament to your commitment to turning ordinary moments into extraordinary memories.

Chapter 8. Harnessing Innovation: Utilizing Technology in Sales

Welcome to the digital frontier of sales, where technology acts as your trusted partner, propelling your efforts to new heights of efficiency, accuracy, and impact. In this dynamic chapter, we'll embark on a journey through the labyrinth of technological possibilities, discovering how to harness innovation to supercharge your sales strategies.

A Symphony of Possibilities

Technology isn't just a tool; it's a symphony of possibilities that can elevate your sales game. From data-driven insights to streamlined communication, the digital realm is your canvas, waiting for you to paint with precision and creativity.

Empowerment through Automation

Imagine automating routine tasks that devour your time and energy. Routine emails, follow-ups, and reminders can be effortlessly managed by software, freeing you to focus on high-impact activities that demand your personal touch.

Navigating the Data Universe

In this age of information, data is your North Star. Technology equips you with the power to analyse customer behaviour, market trends, and competitor insights. By deciphering these patterns, you can tailor your strategies with laser-like precision.

Virtual Handshakes and Global Reach

Distance is no longer a barrier. Virtual meetings and webinars enable you to shake hands with clients across the globe. A well-crafted presentation can now transcend time zones, making your message resonate with audience's continents away.

Customer Relationship Management (CRM): Your Digital Ally

A CRM system isn't just a database; it's a guardian of relationships. It remembers your interactions, tracks leads, and provides insights that help you anticipate customer needs. A CRM transforms cold numbers into warm, thriving connections.

Elevating Customer Experience

Technology isn't just about sales; it's about delivering an unforgettable experience. From interactive websites to chatbots that address inquiries in real time, technology weaves a narrative of customer-centricity, leaving your clients delighted and engaged.

Unleashing Virtual Reality and Augmented Reality

Step into the world of virtual reality and augmented reality. These immersive technologies enable customers to experience products before purchasing, revolutionizing the way you showcase offerings and engage with prospects.

Securing the Castle: Cybersecurity

In this age of digital empowerment, safeguarding sensitive data is paramount. With technology comes the responsibility of robust cybersecurity measures, ensuring both your and your clients' information remains protected.

Conclusion: Guided by Innovation

As you navigate the landscape of technological advancements, remember that technology is your ally, not your replacement. It empowers you to go further, do more, and connect deeper. Embrace this journey with curiosity and courage, for technology isn't just a tool—it's the conduit through which you shape the future of sales.

Navigating the Future: Embracing CRM Systems and Sales Automation

Welcome to a chapter where innovation and human potential converge, creating a symphony of efficiency, organization, and unparalleled customer engagement. In this uplifting exploration, we'll journey through the world of CRM systems and sales automation, discovering how these tools can be your partners in transforming the sales landscape.

Empowering the Sales Journey

Imagine a world where routine tasks are handled seamlessly, leaving you with the freedom to focus on what truly matters: building relationships and closing deals. CRM systems and sales automation are here to grant you that power, ensuring your energy is channelled towards making impactful connections.

Customer Insights: Your North Star

A CRM system is like a treasure trove of insights, waiting to be unlocked. From past interactions to preferences, it transforms data into a compass that guides your interactions, enabling you to tailor your approach and provide unparalleled value to each client.

Seamless Collaboration and Coordination

Sales automation isn't about replacing humans—it's about amplifying human capabilities. With automated workflows and synchronized communication, you can collaborate seamlessly with your team, ensuring everyone is on the same page and every opportunity is maximized.

Personalization at Scale

In the modern world, personalization is the currency of connection. Sales automation allows you to personalize your communication and outreach on a grand scale, ensuring each prospect feels seen, understood, and valued.

Elevating Customer Experience

A well-implemented CRM system is like having a personal assistant who never forgets a detail. From remembering important dates to sending timely follow-ups, it creates an experience that tells your clients they are more than just a transaction.

Focusing on What Matters

Sales automation clears the clutter, allowing you to focus on the essence of your role: nurturing relationships. By handling repetitive tasks, it empowers you to invest your energy in creating meaningful connections that resonate long after the deal is closed.

Predictive Insights: The Crystal Ball of Sales

Imagine having the ability to anticipate your clients' needs. With CRM systems armed with predictive analytics, you can foresee trends, identify opportunities, and be the guiding force in your clients' decision-making journey.

Freedom to Innovate

The beauty of automation is that it liberates you to be creative. It removes the shackles of routine, allowing you to strategize, experiment, and innovate—ultimately shaping the way you engage with clients and elevate your sales approach.

Human Touch in a Digital Age

Amidst all this technology, remember that it's the human touch that adds the magic. A well-implemented CRM system and sales automation aren't replacements; they're enablers, granting you more time to infuse your interactions with empathy, understanding, and authenticity.

Conclusion: Your Symphony of Success

Embrace CRM systems and sales automation with open arms, for they are the instruments that compose your symphony of success. They amplify your potential, orchestrate your efforts, and allow you to create harmonious connections that resonate across the sales landscape. As you embark on this journey, remember that technology is a tool—a tool that, when wielded with intention, empowers you to transcend limitations and embark on a sales journey that is both efficient and profoundly human.

Elevating Your Sales Journey: The Power of social media and Personal Branding

Welcome to a realm where connections are forged, possibilities are limitless, and your unique story takes centre stage. In this uplifting exploration, we'll delve into the transformative world of social media for sales and personal branding—a landscape where authenticity and innovation intertwine to shape a brighter future.

Unleashing Your Potential Through social media

Imagine having a platform that transcends borders and time zones—a space where your voice can be heard by a global audience. Social media is your megaphone, amplifying your message and connecting you with prospects you might have never encountered otherwise.

Creating Your Digital Identity

In the vast digital tapestry, your personal brand is your unique thread. It weaves together your experiences, values, and expertise into a story that resonates with your audience. Craft your personal brand with intention, and watch it become a beacon that guides your sales journey.

Building Trust Through Transparency

In a world where authenticity is currency, social media allows you to showcase the real you. Share your triumphs and challenges, your insights and passions. This transparency humanizes you in the eyes of your audience, fostering trust and relatability.

Crafting Value-Focused Content

Social media isn't just about noise—it's about creating value. Share content that educates, entertains, and resonates with your audience's needs. Whether it's informative articles, inspirational stories, or helpful tips, your content becomes a testament to your commitment to their success.

Engagement: The Heartbeat of Connection

Engagement isn't a mere interaction; it's the heartbeat of a thriving digital community. Respond to comments, engage in conversations, and foster a sense of belonging. Through genuine connections, you'll transform followers into loyal advocates.

Strategic Consistency

Consistency isn't just about showing up—it's about showing up with purpose. Develop a posting schedule that aligns with your audience's online behaviour and your personal brand's narrative. This consistency transforms your presence into a reliable source of inspiration and knowledge.

The Power of Storytelling

Stories have the power to transcend barriers and touch hearts. Use social media to share compelling narratives that showcase your journey, your clients' successes, and the impact of your solutions. Storytelling transforms your message from ordinary to unforgettable.

Leveraging Visuals for Impact

A picture is worth a thousand words, and on social media, visuals are your silent storytellers. Use captivating images, infographics, and videos to create an immersive experience that resonates deeply with your audience.

Community Building: From Connections to Relationships

Beyond numbers, social media is about nurturing a community. Initiate conversations, celebrate milestones, and acknowledge your followers. By turning connections into meaningful relationships, you'll create a tribe that supports your journey.

Conclusion: Your Digital Odyssey

Embrace the world of social media and personal branding as your canvas of creativity and connection. It's not just about technology; it's about infusing your essence into the digital sphere, crafting a symphony of inspiration that resonates far and wide. As you embark on this odyssey, remember that social media isn't a mere tool—it's a stage for your brilliance, a realm where your authenticity shines as a guiding light. May your journey through social media and personal branding be a testament to your unwavering dedication to forging connections, building relationships, and making a meaningful impact in the lives of others.

Embracing Virtual Selling: Navigating the Digital Horizon with Confidence

In the vast landscape of modern sales, a new realm has emerged—one where pixels replace handshakes and screens become the stage for success. Welcome to the world of virtual selling and online platforms, where innovation and connection converge to create a tapestry of endless possibilities.

Redefining Boundaries and Expanding Horizons

Virtual selling transcends borders, enabling you to reach prospects on a global scale from the comfort of your own space. Embrace the idea that your next sale could come from a corner of the world you've never visited—a testament to the power of technology to bridge gaps and open doors.

Creating Immersive Digital Experiences

Online platforms are your canvas for creativity. Craft immersive experiences that engage your audience and transport them into a world where your product or service solves their problems. Through captivating visuals, compelling narratives, and interactive elements, you can make a lasting impact.

Mastering the Art of Connection Through Screens

In a virtual world, your ability to connect remains paramount. Cultivate the art of creating personal connections through screens. Engage with genuine curiosity, listen attentively, and convey your passion and expertise as if you were in the same room.

Empowering Authenticity in the Digital Realm

Authenticity isn't confined to physical spaces—it radiates from within. Embrace your uniqueness and let it shine through your virtual interactions. People connect with real people, so be yourself and let your passion be the driving force that propels your sales journey.

Adapting to the New Rhythm

Virtual selling demands agility and adaptability. Embrace the evolution of the sales process and the new rhythm of virtual interactions. Understand that every click, message, and video call hold the potential to lead you closer to your goals.

Leveraging Technology to Elevate Your Game

Technology is your ally, not your adversary. Utilize sales tools, virtual meeting platforms, and data analytics to enhance your performance. These tools are your toolkit for delivering exceptional value and creating memorable experiences.

Fostering Engagement and Building Trust

Online platforms offer a space to foster engagement and build trust in innovative ways. From webinars that educate to virtual networking events that connect, use the digital landscape to strengthen your relationships and establish yourself as a reliable resource

Nurturing Personalization in a Digital World

The digital sphere doesn't mean losing the personal touch—it means reimagining it. Leverage data to personalize your interactions, tailoring your approach to the unique needs and preferences of each prospect. This demonstrates your dedication to their success, even though screens.

Embracing Resilience and Thriving Digitally

Virtual selling is a journey of resilience and discovery. Embrace the challenges and celebrate the triumphs. As you navigate this digital terrain, remember that your spirit and determination are the fuel that propels you forward.

Conclusion: Unveiling New Horizons

The era of virtual selling isn't just a chapter; it's a revolution. It's a reminder that no matter the circumstances, the human spirit can adapt, innovate, and excel. Embrace the opportunities that online platforms present, and let your sales journey be a testament to the boundless potential of technology to connect hearts, solve problems, and inspire change. May your virtual interactions be as transformative as they are uplifting and may your journey through the digital realm be a beacon of hope, progress, and endless growth.

Chapter 9. Embracing Ethical Excellence: Guiding Light of Professional Sales

In the vast realm of sales, ethics and professionalism shine as beacons of honour and integrity, guiding us through the intricate tapestry of interactions. As you embark on your journey as a sales professional, remember that your actions don't just influence your success, but also the very essence of your character.

The Unshakable Foundation of Trust

Ethical conduct is the cornerstone upon which lasting relationships are built. When you uphold the highest standards of honesty and transparency, you create a foundation of trust that withstands the test of time. Remember that every promise kept, every truth spoken, and every commitment honoured paints a portrait of your integrity.

Navigating the Gray with Unwavering Morality

In the complex landscape of sales, ethical dilemmas can arise. The true test of your character lies in how you navigate these grey areas. Uphold your moral compass with courage, even when the path seems unclear. Trust that doing what is right will always lead you to the right outcome.

Putting People Before Profits

The heart of ethical sales lies in putting people before profits. Your customers aren't mere transactions; they are individuals with unique needs and aspirations. When you approach sales with genuine care for their well-being, you're not just selling a product—you're shaping lives for the better.

The Ripple Effect of Professionalism

Professionalism is the symphony that resonates in every interaction. Your demeanour, communication, and attitude paint a picture of your commitment to excellence. By upholding the highest standards of professionalism, you inspire those around you to reach for their best selves.

Innovation with Integrity

Ethical salesmanship doesn't stifle innovation—it fuels it. Creative solutions can arise without compromising your values. Seek out innovative ways to solve problems, always grounded in your commitment to honesty and ethical conduct.

The Legacy of Positive Impact

In the tapestry of your career, the legacy you weave will be a reflection of your ethical choices. Your influence extends beyond deals closed; it touches lives, shapes industries, and sets the tone for generations to come. Strive to leave a legacy of positive impact that echoes through time.

A Beacon of Integrity

In a world that sometimes seems fraught with shortcuts and compromises, your commitment to ethics and professionalism shines as a beacon of light. Embrace the role of an ethical sales professional with pride, knowing that your choices uplift not only your career but also the very essence of the sales profession.

Conclusion: Illuminating the Path Ahead

Sales ethics and professionalism are not mere concepts; they are the essence of what it means to be a true sales professional. Let these principles guide you through the labyrinth of opportunities and challenges, inspiring you to always choose the path of honour and integrity. May your commitment to ethical excellence illuminate the path ahead, lighting the way for others to follow, and may your journey through the world of sales be a testament to the power of ethical conduct to shape not just your success, but your character.

Upholding the Torch of Ethical Excellence: Your Guiding Light in Sales

In the world of sales, where opportunities and challenges intermingle, maintaining unwavering ethical standards stands as a testament to your character and integrity. As you navigate the intricate dance of transactions and relationships, remember that your commitment to ethics doesn't just define your actions—it defines who you are.

The Power of Integrity

Ethical standards are the cornerstone of any successful sales career. They're not mere guidelines; they're the embodiment of your integrity. When you choose honesty over deception and transparency over ambiguity, you project a powerful image of trustworthiness that resonates with customers, colleagues, and partners alike.

Walking the Ethical Tightrope

In the labyrinth of sales, there might be moments when the line between right and wrong seems blurred. These moments become the ultimate tests of your character. When you choose to follow the path of ethics, even in the face of temptation, you showcase your unwavering commitment to doing what's right—no matter the circumstances.

The Ripple Effect of Ethical Leadership

Your ethical choices reverberate beyond individual transactions. They shape the way you're perceived by your peers, managers, and clients. By consistently adhering to ethical standards, you become a beacon of leadership that inspires others to follow in your footsteps, creating a collective culture of integrity.

Balancing Profits with Principles

Contrary to misconception, ethical standards don't hinder success—they enhance it. The long-term gains of a reputation built on integrity far outweigh the short-lived profits from questionable practices. Remember that when you prioritize ethics, you're laying the foundation for sustainable success and enduring relationships.

Ethical Decision-Making: Your North Star

Ethical standards serve as your North Star in moments of uncertainty. When faced with difficult decisions, ask yourself: "Is this aligned with my values? Would I be proud of this choice if it were public?" Let your commitment to ethics guide you, and you'll emerge from any challenge with your integrity intact.

Creating a Legacy of Integrity

Every action you take, every choice you make, contributes to the legacy you're creating. As you weave your way through the world of sales, consider the legacy you want to leave behind. Let it be one of unwavering integrity—a legacy that future generations can look up to and aspire towards.

Embracing the Hero's Journey

In your sales journey, ethics is your hero's armour. It's what sets you apart, what ensures you rise above the noise, and what empowers you to become a true advocate for your clients. Embrace this journey with enthusiasm, knowing that every ethical decision is a step towards your own greatness.

Conclusion: Radiating Ethical Brilliance

Maintaining ethical standards in sales isn't just a requirement; it's a reflection of your commitment to excellence. As you progress in your career, remember that the choices you make ripple through time, influencing the lives of countless individuals. Embrace your role as a guardian of ethical excellence, knowing that your commitment to integrity not only defines your sales journey but also leaves an indelible mark on the world.

Embracing the Beacon of Transparency: Illuminating Pathways to Trust

In the heart of every successful customer interaction lies the radiant flame of transparency and honesty. These virtues are not mere attributes; they're the foundation upon which you build lasting relationships and forge unbreakable bonds. As you navigate the labyrinth of customer interactions, remember that transparency isn't just a tactic—it's a beacon that guides you towards the pinnacle of trust.

Transparency: The Bridge to Authenticity

When you choose transparency, you're choosing authenticity. You're opening the door to genuine connections by allowing your customers a glimpse into your world. Transparent communication transforms you from a salesperson into a trusted ally, someone who is willing to share insights, challenges, and victories without reservation.

The Power of Honesty

Honesty is a force that transcends transactional boundaries. It's not just about admitting when something goes wrong; it's about being forthright even when it's uncomfortable. When you're honest, you show that you value your customer's time, intelligence, and trust—a gesture that resonates deeply and sets the stage for profound relationships.

A Journey of Discovery

Transparency and honesty turn each interaction into a journey of discovery. As you unveil the intricacies of your offerings, share the details of your process, and lay bare the benefits and potential challenges, you invite your customers to embark on a shared voyage of exploration. Through this journey, you empower them to make informed decisions that align with their needs and aspirations.

Beyond the Transaction: Building Loyalty

In the world of sales, your commitment to transparency extends beyond the initial transaction. It's a pledge to be available for questions, concerns, and updates. By staying engaged and maintaining open lines of communication, you create an environment where customers know they can count on you even after the deal is done.

Transparency as Empowerment

Transparency isn't about showcasing perfection; it's about fostering empowerment. When you're open about what your product or service can and cannot deliver, you empower customers to make choices that truly serve their interests. This empowerment is a testament to your commitment to their success, strengthening the bonds of trust.

Trust: The Currency of Lasting Relationships

In the realm of sales, trust is the most precious currency. It's built on the foundation of transparency and honesty, and it's what transforms a single transaction into a lifelong partnership. The trust you cultivate with your customers today becomes the bedrock of referrals, repeat business, and a legacy of excellence.

Creating a Culture of Truth

Transparency and honesty aren't fleeting actions; they're the cornerstones of a culture you foster. When you prioritize truthfulness, you inspire others to do the same. Your example ripples through your team, your organization, and even beyond, creating a collective commitment to ethical and genuine interactions.

Conclusion: Illuminating the Pathway

As you step into each customer interaction, embrace the radiant power of transparency and honesty. Let these virtues guide you towards building relationships that transcend transactions. With every word you speak and action you take, remember that you're not just selling—you're igniting a beacon of trust that lights the way for both you and your customers.

Long-Term Relationships: Nurturing the Seeds of Success

In the bustling world of sales, the choice between short-term gains and long-term relationships is akin to deciding between instant gratification and cultivating a thriving garden. Let's explore this dynamic as you navigate the lush terrain of lasting connections and the allure of immediate victories.

The Temptation of Quick Wins

Short-term goals often beckon like shiny trinkets, promising swift gratification. While they can inject a burst of energy into your journey, they're like shooting stars—here one moment, gone the next. These wins might bring a momentary glow, but their brilliance can fade as quickly as it emerged.

Cultivating a Garden of Trust

On the other hand, long-term relationships resemble a garden you carefully tend. Each interaction is a seed sown, nurtured, and eventually blossoming into a resilient plant. These connections are built on trust, nurtured through consistent care, and weather the storms of challenges. They become a source of stability, providing shade on scorching days and beauty in every season.

The Symphony of Trust and Loyalty

Picture your sales journey as a symphony, with each long-term relationship as a note that contributes to the harmony. The melodies of trust and loyalty intertwine, creating a masterpiece that resonates far beyond short-lived accolades. It's in these relationships that you find the rhythm of enduring success.

Beyond Transactions: Creating Legacies

When you opt for short-term goals, you may focus solely on the transaction at hand. But when you invest in long-term relationships, you're crafting legacies. You're leaving imprints of your authenticity, your commitment, and your value. These legacies reverberate even when the deal is done, building bridges to future opportunities.

The Tapestry of Loyalty

Imagine your journey as a tapestry, woven with threads of interactions, engagements, and shared successes. Each long-term relationship adds a vibrant hue to this tapestry, making it a mosaic of experiences and accomplishments. As you weave these threads, you create a portrait of not just a salesperson, but a trusted advisor, a confidant, and a partner.

Striking the Balance

While short-term wins can give you a taste of success, long-term relationships offer a feast of fulfilment. Striking the balance is key—leveraging quick victories to fuel your momentum while tending to the long-term connections that form the backbone of your journey. It's in this equilibrium that you sculpt a story of achievements, both immediate and enduring.

Conclusion: The Legacy of Connection

As you stand at the crossroads of short-term goals and long-term relationships, remember that you're not just making decisions for today; you're shaping your legacy. The impact of your actions reaches beyond numbers and spreadsheets; it touches lives, influences businesses, and forms lasting bonds. So, let the allure of immediate success be a steppingstone, leading you to the garden of lasting relationships. With each interaction, you're not just achieving sales—you're weaving a legacy of connection, trust, and prosperity that resonates through time.

Chapter 10. Unveiling the Tapestry of Success: Exploring Sales Metrics and Performance Measurement

Welcome to a realm where numbers are not just digits; they're the threads that weave the tapestry of success. In Chapter 10, we delve into the intricate world of sales metrics and performance measurement—a realm where every data point is a brushstroke on the canvas of achievement. Here, we transcend the surface and journey into the heart of understanding what drives our progress, and how we can harness these insights to propel ourselves further.

Beneath the Surface: The Story Numbers Tell

Sales metrics are the storytellers of your journey. They reveal the narrative of your efforts—the victories, challenges, and areas for growth. These metrics are not mere statistics; they're the compass that guides your decisions, enabling you to navigate the terrain of your sales landscape with precision.

The Symphony of Performance Measurement

In this chapter, we're not just crunching numbers; we're composing a symphony of performance measurement. Each metric plays a distinct role—a note in the melody of your sales strategy. As we explore conversion rates, customer acquisition costs, pipeline velocity, and more, you'll begin to see how these measures harmonize to create the grand opus of your sales success.

From Data to Wisdom

Data, when harnessed with intention, transforms into wisdom. Our journey takes us beyond the surface-level interpretations of numbers and into the realm of deep analysis. We'll unearth patterns, identify trends, and unlock insights that illuminate the pathways to enhanced performance and growth.

A Toolkit for Success

Think of this chapter as your toolkit for success—a set of finely honed instruments that enable you to measure, analyse, and optimize. Armed with the right metrics, you'll not only understand where you stand but also discern the strategies and tactics that lead to triumph.

Navigating the Sea of Metrics

In a sea of data, it's easy to feel overwhelmed. But fear not, for this chapter will be your compass, guiding you towards the metrics that truly matter. We'll explore the balance between leading and lagging indicators, and how each contributes to your understanding of progress and direction.

Elevating Your Performance

The beauty of sales metrics is their capacity to elevate your performance. They're the mirrors that reflect your strengths and expose your blind spots. Armed with these insights, you'll have the power to fine-tune your approach, make informed decisions, and, ultimately, amplify your impact.

Conclusion: Numbers with a Purpose

As we embark on this journey through the realm of sales metrics and performance measurement, remember that these numbers aren't just cold figures—they're the heartbeat of your success. With each metric we explore, you'll uncover the pulse of your efforts and gain the wisdom to steer your journey towards greater achievements. So, let's dive in, not as spectators but as explorers of the vast landscape where data intertwines with purpose, and numbers paint a portrait of victory.

Guiding the Way: Unveiling the Magic of Key Performance Indicators (KPIs)

Imagine KPIs as your guiding stars in the constellation of sales success. They're not just numbers; they're the luminous points that illuminate your path and reveal the treasures hidden within your efforts. In this section, we'll embark on a journey to decode the magic of Key Performance Indicators—the compass that ensures you're headed in the right direction.

The Significance of KPIs

KPIs are the heartbeat of your sales strategy. They're the instruments that translate your ambitions into measurable objectives. With KPIs, you don't just set sail blindly; you chart a course towards defined goals, steering with clarity and purpose.

A Symphony of Measurement

Think of KPIs as the different notes that come together to create a symphony of success. From conversion rates and customer lifetime value to sales growth and lead-to-deal ratios, each KPI is a distinct tune that, when orchestrated skilfully, produces a harmonious composition of achievement.

Choosing Your Constellation

In the vast cosmos of KPIs, you'll find a constellation that's unique to your goals. Just as sailors navigate using constellations, you'll navigate your sales journey with specific KPIs that align with your objectives. Whether it's revenue targets, customer retention rates, or sales cycle duration, each KPI guides you towards your destination.

Leading and Lagging Stars

KPIs come in two flavours: leading and lagging. Leading KPIs act as your guiding stars, signalling what actions you need to take to achieve your goals. Lagging KPIs, on the other hand, shine light on the outcomes of those actions. Balancing both is the key to a well-rounded perspective of your sales performance.

Beyond the Surface

KPIs go beyond the surface; they're a portal into the depth of your strategies. When you study your KPIs, you're not just looking at numbers— you're deciphering the story behind those numbers. Are your conversion rates dropping due to changes in your pitch? Is your customer acquisition cost rising because of increased competition? KPIs reveal these narratives, enabling you to make informed decisions.

Measuring Your North Star

Just as explorers relied on the North Star for guidance, KPIs provide you with a constant reference point. When the seas get rough and the journey challenging, KPIs remind you of your true north—the goals you've set and the progress you're making. They prevent you from veering off course and empower you to stay on track.

Conclusion: Your Guiding Light

As you navigate the galaxies of sales, let KPIs be your guiding light. They're not just numbers on a dashboard; they're the celestial guides that illuminate your way. With each KPI you set and measure, you're crafting a map to success, ensuring that every step you take is aligned with your aspirations. So, embrace the magic of Key Performance Indicators, and let them be the constellations that lead you towards the bright horizon of your sales journey.

Elevate Your Success: The Art of Evaluating Sales Performance and Setting Aims

In the vibrant tapestry of sales, evaluating performance and setting goals are the threads that weave your journey towards achievement. Picture this section as your compass, guiding you through the exhilarating landscape of progress assessment and goal creation.

The Dance of Evaluation

Evaluation is not a cold, clinical task; it's a dance with your accomplishments. It's a celebration of your wins and a graceful examination of areas that beckon improvement. Just as a choreographer refines a dance, you refine your strategies, ensuring each step is in perfect harmony with your objectives.

The Mirrors of Metrics

Metrics are your mirrors, reflecting the truth of your efforts. But they're not there to critique; they're there to inspire growth. Metrics are your allies, showing you where you shine and where you can polish your brilliance. When you assess your metrics, you're not just looking at numbers; you're gazing into the pool of potential, ready to dive into greater achievements.

Embrace Every Step

Remember, the path of evaluation is not just about the destination; it's about embracing each step you take. The moments when you stumble teach you resilience, and the leaps forward fill you with exhilaration. Every challenge you face is an opportunity for growth, a chance to ascend higher and reach new heights.

Setting Sail Towards Goals

Setting goals is like setting sail on an ocean of possibilities. Goals are the stars that guide your ship towards uncharted territories. They're the milestones that mark your progress and the lighthouses that keep you from straying off course. Whether it's conquering a new market, surpassing last year's revenue, or expanding your client base, goals are your compass, pointing you towards success.

The Canvas of Vision

Think of goal setting as an artist's canvas. It's where you paint the picture of your future, each stroke representing an aspiration, a dream, and a commitment. As you add layers to your canvas, your masterpiece takes shape. With each goal set, you're adding vibrant hues of determination, dedication, and drive.

Growth as a Guiding Principle

Embrace the idea that growth is not just an endgame; it's a guiding principle. Each evaluation and goal you undertake is a testament to your commitment to self-improvement. It's a declaration that you're not content withstanding still; you're destined to evolve, to flourish, and to create ripples of success that touch every corner of your sales journey.

Conclusion: Unveiling Your Potential

As you dive into the sea of evaluating performance and setting goals, remember that you're not just shaping your career—you're shaping your destiny. Let the dance of evaluation and goal setting be a symphony of inspiration, guiding you towards the crescendo of achievement. With each step you take, you're unveiling your potential, expanding your horizons, and crafting a story of success that's uniquely yours. So, embrace the journey, welcome the challenges, and let the magic of evaluation and goal setting lift you higher than you ever imagined.

Evolving Brilliance: The Journey of Continuous Improvement

In the ever-evolving landscape of sales, the path of progress is paved with the bricks of continuous improvement. Much like a sculptor refining their masterpiece, you have the power to chisel away the rough edges of your skills and knowledge, revealing the brilliance that lies beneath. Let's embark on this journey of growth and enlightenment.

Unveiling Your Potential

Imagine your skills and knowledge as a treasure trove waiting to be unearthed. Every interaction, every challenge, and every lesson is a brushstroke that reveals a clearer picture of your potential. But unlike a static masterpiece, your brilliance isn't fixed. It's dynamic, adapting and evolving as you seek to refine your craft.

The Art of Adaptation

Just as a painter adjusts their palette to capture the nuances of a changing landscape, you too must adapt. Sales techniques that worked yesterday might need a fresh perspective today. The magic lies in your ability to identify these shifts and embrace them with open arms, constantly refining your approach.

Growth Through Feedback

Think of feedback as the sculptor's chisel, helping you chip away at imperfections. It might sting at first, but remember that every critique, every suggestion, is a chance to shape a better version of yourself. Embrace feedback as a guiding light toward your highest potential.

The Tapestry of Learning

In your journey of continuous improvement, you weave a tapestry of learning experiences. Every course you take, every book you read, every workshop you attend—they're all threads that add depth and complexity to your narrative. This tapestry isn't just a collection of certificates; it's a story of your dedication to growth.

Embracing Curiosity

A curious mind is an open gateway to growth. Approach each day with the spirit of a curious explorer, ready to unravel new insights and unravel uncharted territories. The more you explore, the more you expand your horizons, enriching your toolbox with diverse perspectives.

Rising Above Comfort Zones

Much like a climber pushing beyond the familiar terrain, you must step outside your comfort zones. It's in these uncharted territories that you'll discover your latent abilities, hidden talents, and untapped potential. Embrace discomfort as a sign that you're on the cusp of something extraordinary.

Conclusion: A Symphony of Progress

In the grand symphony of your sales journey, the notes of continuous improvement harmonize with each achievement, each lesson, and each experience. Your commitment to evolving brilliance transforms routine into innovation, mediocrity into excellence, and good into exceptional. As you navigate the cadence of change, remember that growth isn't a one-time destination; it's a lifelong expedition.

So, nurture your thirst for knowledge, embrace the winds of change, and revel in the pursuit of constant betterment. With each step forward, you're painting a masterpiece of your own evolution—a canvas that celebrates not just what you've accomplished, but who you're becoming. May your journey of continuous improvement be a symphony of progress, resonating through the realms of success and beyond.

Chapter 11. Navigating Diverse Horizons: Adapting to Different Selling Environments

In the exhilarating landscape of sales, one truth prevails: adaptability is the compass that guides you through a world of diverse selling environments. Just as a seasoned traveller adjusts their sails to the wind's whims, so must you adapt your strategies to the unique contours of each selling environment. As we embark on this chapter, prepare to learn the art of versatility—a skill that will enable you to thrive wherever your sales journey takes you.

Embracing the Kaleidoscope of Opportunities

Imagine the sales world as a sprawling terrain, each environment a unique ecosystem waiting to be explored. From the boardrooms of corporate giants to the bustling bazaars of small businesses, every setting comes with its own rhythm, expectations, and challenges. And like an adaptable chameleon, you have the remarkable ability to blend into each backdrop while retaining your authenticity.

The Shape-Shifting Salesperson

Just as a skilled actor can seamlessly switch roles on stage, a successful salesperson adeptly shifts between diverse selling environments. Your power lies in your versatility—a knack for understanding the dynamics of each context and moulding your approach accordingly. The secret? Honouring the essence of your sales philosophy while tailoring it to resonate with the unique heartbeat of your audience.

The Symphony of Cultural Intelligence

Picture yourself as a maestro conducting an orchestra of interactions. Different selling environments often come with varied cultural nuances. Being attuned to these subtleties, much like interpreting the intricate notes of a melody, enables you to strike chords of understanding and forge connections that transcend borders.

The Architect of Flexibility

Think of yourself as an architect of flexibility, constructing bridges between your strategies and the selling environment's demands. Just as a building's blueprint adapts to its surroundings, your sales approach shifts to create the strongest connection with your audience. Flexibility isn't a compromise; it's the glue that binds your authenticity to your adaptability.

Becoming an Ethereal Navigator

In the realm of diverse selling environments, you're not merely a salesperson; you're an ethereal navigator, navigating through the winds of change with grace and acumen. Whether you're presenting in a sleek office, networking at a lively event, or conversing one-on-one in a cozy café, your ability to adapt is the wind beneath your wings.

Conclusion: The Dance of Adaptation

As we delve into the art of adapting to different selling environments, remember that versatility isn't about compromising your identity—it's about enhancing it. Like a diamond reflecting myriad colours under different lights, your skills and strategies shine brightest when tailored to the context. With each encounter, you're crafting a mosaic of adaptability, a mosaic that's as unique as it is effective.

So, embark on this exploration with an open heart and an agile mind. Embrace each new environment as an opportunity to learn, to connect, and to evolve. As you dance through diverse landscapes, remember that your adaptability isn't just a skill; it's a testament to your resilience and growth. May your journey through various selling environments be a vibrant tapestry of connections, illuminating the path to your sales success.

Harmonizing Strategies: B2B vs. B2C Sales in Perfect Balance

In the realm of sales, two dynamic approaches shine: Business-to-Business (B2B) and Business-to-Consumer (B2C) strategies. Each carries its own unique rhythm, offering a chance to create resonance in different ways. This section is your gateway to understanding and embracing these strategies, allowing you to weave success stories regardless of the audience you're engaging with.

B2B: Nurturing Partnerships and Growth

Imagine B2B strategies as crafting a garden where collaboration flourishes. Here, the art lies in cultivating relationships and fostering growth together. It's like planting seeds of trust and tending to them as they bloom into mutually beneficial partnerships. B2B sales aren't just transactions; they're journeys of teamwork and shared victories.

B2C: Crafting Personal Connections

In the realm of B2C, envision creating a unique painting, each brushstroke portraying an individual story. B2C sales are about tapping into emotions, resonating with needs, and offering tailored solutions. It's like understanding the colours that make up a person's life and using them to paint a canvas of connection.

Where Both Strategies Converge

Even though B2B and B2C might seem like different roads, they share common values. Just as a warm smile is universally understood, both strategies require authenticity, understanding, and value. Think of them as two rivers meeting at a point—your expertise helps them blend into a powerful stream of success.

Finding the Beauty in B2B2C

Picture a tapestry where threads of B2B and B2C weave together, forming an intricate pattern. This is B2B2C, where partnerships create pathways for individual delight. Imagine a tech provider partnering with a retailer to enhance customer journeys. In this realm, you're not just selling; you're curating experiences.

Embrace the Possibilities

As you explore B2B and B2C strategies, remember that every interaction you have adds to a bigger narrative. Whether you're nurturing partnerships in the B2B world or building individual connections in B2C, you're contributing to a vibrant tapestry of commerce. Your ability to understand, empathize, and adapt is the brush that paints a bright future.

So, step into this realm with an open heart and a curious spirit. The balance of B2B and B2C is your playground, where you dance to the rhythm of human connections and potential growth. May your journey through these strategies be uplifting, allowing you to create harmonious sales stories that brighten lives and light up success.

Exploring Inside Sales and Field Sales: Unveiling Two Paths to Success

In the realm of sales, there are two distinct paths that professional's traverse: the dynamic world of inside sales and the adventurous domain of field sales. Each path has its own rhythm and rewards, offering unique opportunities for success. Let's dive into the intriguing dance of Inside Sales and Field Sales, discovering the nuances that make each journey extraordinary.

Inside Sales: The Art of Virtual Engagement

Imagine yourself in the heart of a bustling metropolis, surrounded by screens and technology. Welcome to the realm of Inside Sales, where the virtual world becomes your canvas for connection. Here, you master the art of engaging with clients and prospects through digital channels. The hum of a phone call, the click of a mouse, and the glow of a screen are your instruments.

The Power of Reach and Efficiency

Inside Sales offers a wide reach and swift efficiency. You're able to connect with a global audience at the tap of a button. With technology as your ally, you navigate through diverse time zones, cultures, and industries, all from the comfort of your workspace. Your voice carries across distances, forging connections that transcend geography.

Field Sales: The Journey of Face-to-Face Connections

Now, picture yourself on a journey across landscapes, meeting people in person and shaking hands on foreign grounds. Welcome to Field Sales, where every meeting is an adventure, and every handshake is a pact. In this realm, you become the embodiment of your product, delivering your message with the full force of your presence.

The Magic of Personal Interaction

Field Sales is all about the magic of personal interaction. The authenticity of a firm handshake, the warmth of eye contact, and the resonance of your voice create a symphony of trust. You build relationships not only with your words but with your body language, your expressions, and the genuine connections you forge on the road.

Balancing the Scales: Both Have Their Merits

Inside Sales and Field Sales are two sides of the same coin, each with its own merits. Inside Sales excels in speed and accessibility, allowing you to cover vast ground with a few clicks. Field Sales shines in its ability to create lasting impressions through face-to-face meetings, leveraging the power of human connection.

Choosing Your Path

As you contemplate your sales journey, remember that there's no one-size-fits-all approach. Your personality, strengths, and aspirations will guide you towards the path that resonates with you. Some thrive in the bustling virtual landscape of Inside Sales, while others find their calling in the adventure of Field Sales.

A World of Possibilities

Inside Sales and Field Sales are not separate worlds; they're interconnected chapters in the ever-evolving book of sales. Regardless of the path you choose, remember that your mission remains the same: to create value, build relationships, and make a positive impact. Whether you're navigating digital landscapes or traversing physical terrains, may your journey be one of growth, success, and meaningful connections.

Embracing Global Harmony: Navigating Cross-Cultural Sales

In a world as diverse as ours, the realm of sales extends beyond borders, transcending cultures and languages. Welcome to the realm of global and cross-cultural sales, where understanding and respect become your compass, guiding you through the vibrant tapestry of international business. Here, success is not only about closing deals but also about building bridges that connect hearts and minds.

The Melody of Diversity

Imagine global sales as a grand symphony where every culture brings its unique instruments. Each note represents a cultural nuance, and the harmonious blend of these notes creates a mesmerizing composition. Just as a conductor orchestrates a symphony, your role in global sales is to navigate the diverse harmonies and bring them together in a melodious arrangement.

Cultural Intelligence: Your Secret Weapon

In this realm, cultural intelligence is your most valuable asset. Think of it as a passport to the hearts of your clients and partners around the world. It's the art of understanding cultural nuances, gestures, values, and communication styles. When you embrace cultural intelligence, you become a global citizen, capable of speaking the language of trust and understanding.

Creating Bridges, Not Boundaries

Cross-cultural sales are about weaving bridges that span continents, cultures, and perspectives. Just as a bridge connects two shores, your approach should connect your clients' needs and aspirations with your products and services. This isn't just business; it's about fostering mutual growth, respect, and shared successes.

Cultivating Empathy and Flexibility

Picture yourself as a traveller embarking on a journey through different landscapes. As you navigate these terrains, empathy and flexibility become your compass. Embrace the beauty of differences and cultivate empathy for your clients' unique challenges. Be flexible in adapting your strategies to accommodate different cultural preferences.

Learning and Growing Together

In this vibrant global marketplace, each interaction is a learning opportunity. Just as a new language enriches your vocabulary, every cross-cultural engagement enriches your understanding. As you collaborate with people from diverse backgrounds, you gain insights that expand your worldview and refine your approach.

The Universal Language of Respect

No matter the culture or language, respect is the universal language of success. Treat each interaction as a chance to build bridges of respect and understanding. A sincere handshake, a bow, or a warm smile—all express your intention to connect authentically.

Step into the Global Arena

As you venture into the world of global and cross-cultural sales, remember that you're not just a salesperson; you're an ambassador of connections. Every deal you close is a chord in the symphony of international commerce. May your journey through diverse cultures be filled with curiosity, empathy, and respect, and may your ability to bridge gaps lead you to a realm of global success and meaningful relationships.

Chapter 12. Mastering Time Management and Productivity in the World of Sales

In the exhilarating dance of sales, time is your currency, and productivity is your rhythm. As you navigate through a dynamic landscape of tasks, interactions, and opportunities, the ability to manage your time wisely becomes paramount. Welcome to the chapter dedicated to unlocking the secrets of Time Management and Productivity in Sales—a journey that empowers you to make the most of every moment.

The Symphony of Prioritization

Imagine yourself as the conductor of an orchestra, determining which notes to emphasize and when. In the realm of sales, prioritization is your baton. Effective time management starts with identifying the tasks that carry the most weight in achieving your goals. Just as a conductor highlights key melodies, you allocate your time to high-impact activities that drive results.

The Dance of Focus and Distraction

Picture yourself as a skilled dancer on a bustling stage, gracefully moving through your routines. In sales, focus is your choreography, and distractions are the noise of the audience. To excel, you must master the art of maintaining focus on your tasks amidst the sea of distractions. Whether it's the ping of notifications or the allure of unrelated tasks, your ability to stay centred shapes your performance.

Redefining Multitasking

In the whirlwind of sales, multitasking is often hailed as a skill. However, think of it as juggling—trying to keep multiple balls in the air simultaneously. In reality, focusing on one task at a time increases efficiency and quality. Instead of juggling, consider dancing between tasks with purpose, dedicating your attention fully to each one before gracefully transitioning to the next.

Creating Rituals of Efficiency

Envision yourself as an artisan crafting a masterpiece. Your canvas is your work environment, and your tools are your rituals. Rituals, such as starting your day with a clear plan, scheduling focused work blocks, and taking intentional breaks, create an environment of efficiency. These rituals ensure that you're consistently in the flow, moving seamlessly from one task to the next.

The Symphony of Self-Care

Just as a musician must care for their instrument, you must care for yourself. The harmony of time management includes nurturing your well-being. Regular exercise, healthy meals, and moments of rejuvenation compose the symphony of self-care. When you are in peak physical and mental condition, your productivity soars to new heights.

Embracing Technology as Your Conductor's Baton

Imagine technology as your conductor's baton, guiding your movements. In the digital age, technology offers an array of tools to optimize time management. From task management apps to calendar systems, these digital assistants keep you in rhythm, ensuring that no opportunity is missed, and no task falls through the cracks.

A Symphony of Achievement

As you navigate the sales landscape, remember that time is your canvas, and productivity is your masterpiece. Every moment is a brushstroke, contributing to the vibrant picture of your success. Whether you're composing the symphony of prioritization, perfecting the dance of focus, or crafting rituals of efficiency, your commitment to time management and productivity orchestrates a symphony of achievement.

Embrace the art of harmonizing your time, and let your productivity resonate like a beautiful melody in the realm of sales. With every task mastered and every goal achieved, may your journey be a symphony of success, with time itself applauding your achievements.

Crafting the Path: Planning and Organizing Your Sales Activities

In the bustling world of sales, where every interaction holds the promise of success, planning and organization emerge as your guiding lights. Think of yourself as a skilled navigator charting a course through uncharted waters, with a map crafted from careful planning and a compass composed of organizational finesse. Welcome to the realm of Planning and Organizing Sales Activities—a journey that transforms chaos into order, and aspirations into achievements.

Sketching the Blueprint

Imagine embarking on a journey without a map—the path forward would be uncertain, and the destination vague. In sales, your blueprint is your plan—an intricate design that outlines your objectives, strategies, and timelines. Just as an architect conceptualizes a building, your plan is the foundation upon which your success rests. By plotting your course with clarity, you pave the way for a purposeful journey.

The Art of Prioritization

Picture yourself as a curator selecting gems for an exhibition. In sales, your gems are your tasks, each with its own value and impact. Effective planning is the art of prioritization, where you identify the high-value tasks that drive your success. Like a curator choosing the most precious jewels, you allocate your time and resources to the tasks that align with your goals, ensuring that your efforts yield the most valuable results.

Weaving a Web of Strategy

Envision yourself as a weaver crafting a tapestry, intertwining threads to create a masterpiece. In sales, your tapestry is your strategy—a complex interplay of actions that leads to triumph. A well-structured strategy aligns your activities with your objectives, ensuring that each step contributes to your larger goal. Just as a weaver selects threads for their colour and texture, you craft a strategy that weaves together activities of purpose and impact.

The Symphony of Time Management

Think of yourself as a conductor leading an orchestra, orchestrating the sequence of tasks with finesse. Time management is your baton, ensuring that each note is played at the right moment. Effective organization of your activities allows you to glide seamlessly through your day, transitioning from task to task without missing a beat. By conducting your time with precision, you create a symphony of productivity and accomplishment.

Navigating with Precision

Imagine yourself as an explorer navigating through uncharted terrain, meticulously marking each step. In sales, your journey is guided by meticulous organization, ensuring that no opportunity is overlooked, and no task is forgotten. Whether it's tracking leads, scheduling follow-ups, or preparing for meetings, your organizational prowess transforms you into an efficient trailblazer, leaving no stone unturned in your quest for success.

Creating Your Masterpiece

As you embark on your sales journey, remember that planning and organization are the canvases upon which your success is painted. Just as an artist brings life to their masterpiece through deliberate strokes, you bring life to your goals through purposeful planning and meticulous organization. Your roadmap becomes a masterpiece of achievements, a gallery of fulfilled aspirations.

Craft the path, map the course, and orchestrate the journey—may you're planning, and organizational skills transform your sales endeavours into a symphony of accomplishment. With every activity meticulously managed and every goal strategically pursued, may your journey be a testament to the power of planning and the beauty of organized execution.

Chapter 13. Guiding Stars: Navigating Sales Leadership and Team Management

In the realm of sales, leadership is the North Star that illuminates the path to success. Imagine standing at the helm of a ship, steering your team toward uncharted horizons. Welcome to the world of Sales Leadership and Team Management—a journey where you don the captain's hat, guiding your crew through turbulent waters toward the shores of triumph.

Leading with Purpose

Picture a conductor on a grand stage, leading a symphony with precision and passion. In sales leadership, you are that conductor, guiding your team toward harmonious success. Your leadership shapes the orchestra of talents under your command, orchestrating their skills to create a symphony of achievement. Just as a conductor sets the tempo, your leadership sets the pace for your team's journey to excellence.

Forging Strong Bonds

Imagine a weaver crafting a tapestry, blending threads of various colours and textures into a harmonious whole. In team management, you are the weaver, intertwining the diverse strengths of your team members into a cohesive unit. Your leadership forges bonds of camaraderie and mutual support, creating a tapestry of collaboration that enhances the overall fabric of success.

Nurturing Growth

Envision a gardener tending to a garden, nurturing each plant with care to ensure abundant growth. In sales leadership, you are the gardener, cultivating the talents of your team members. Your guidance provides the nourishment they need to bloom and flourish. Like a gardener who prunes to encourage growth, you empower your team through mentorship and skill development, fostering a culture of continuous improvement.

Empowering Through Vision

Think of a lighthouse that guides ships through the darkness, offering a beacon of hope and direction. In sales leadership, your vision is that guiding light, inspiring your team to sail toward shared goals. Your clear vision provides direction, helping your team navigate through challenges and uncertainties. Like a lighthouse, your leadership illuminates the way, showing your team the path to success.

Fostering Resilience

Imagine a coach on the sidelines, cheering on their team through victories and setbacks. In sales leadership, you are that coach, fostering resilience in the face of challenges. Your unwavering support and guidance instil a sense of confidence and determination in your team. Just as a coach helps players rebound from defeats, you inspire your team to learn and grow from their experiences.

Creating a Legacy

As you step into the realm of sales leadership and team management, remember that your role is not just about directing tasks—it's about shaping futures. Just as a captain charts the course of a ship, you steer your team toward success. With every decision you make and every example you set, you are sculpting a legacy of empowered individuals and collective achievement.

Lead with purpose, forge strong bonds, nurture growth, empower through vision, and foster resilience—may your journey through sales leadership and team management be one of inspiration and transformation. With each step, may you guide your team to new heights of success, crafting a legacy of collaboration, growth, and unwavering dedication to excellence.

Transitioning from Salesperson to Sales Manager

Elevating Horizons: Transitioning from Salesperson to Sales Manager

Imagine a soaring eagle, rising above the clouds to embrace a broader perspective. Such is the journey of transitioning from a salesperson to a sales manager—a transformative ascent that takes you from the realm of individual contribution to the summit of leadership and guidance.

Embracing Your New Role

Picture a conductor stepping onto the podium, ready to lead a magnificent orchestra. As you transition to a sales manager, you step into a role where your guidance orchestrates the collective talents of your team. Your ability to harmonize these talents into a symphony of success will determine the melody that resonates through your department.

Nurturing Future Leaders

Think of a gardener tending to a garden, not just for today's blooms but for the blossoms of tomorrow. As a sales manager, your role is akin to that gardener, nurturing the growth of your team members. Your guidance and mentorship cultivate not only their skills but also their potential as future leaders. Just as a garden flourishes with care, your team will thrive under your tutelage.

Empowering Others

Imagine a skilled craftsman, shaping raw materials into a masterpiece. In your new role, you become that craftsman, moulding the raw potential of your team into a cohesive force. Your empowerment creates an environment where each team member's strengths are harnessed to drive collective success. Just as a craftsman crafts with intention, your leadership shapes the future of your team.

Navigating Challenges

Think of a ship's captain, guiding the vessel through stormy waters with a steady hand. As a sales manager, your leadership is like that captain's guidance. You steer your team through challenges, providing stability and direction. Your resilience in the face of adversity sets an example, inspiring your team to navigate through any obstacle.

Cultivating a Collaborative Culture

Envision a weaver creating a tapestry, intricately blending threads of diverse colours. In your new role, you are that weaver, uniting your team's diverse skills into a harmonious whole. Your ability to foster collaboration nurtures an atmosphere of shared goals and mutual support. Like a tapestry, your team becomes a beautiful mosaic of talents working together.

Crafting Your Legacy

As you transition from a salesperson to a sales manager, you embark on a journey of transformation and growth. Remember that your new role is not just about managing tasks; it's about shaping futures. Your leadership influences not only the success of your team but also the trajectory of their individual careers. With each decision you make and each example you set, you are crafting a legacy of empowered individuals and collective achievement.

Embrace your new role with an open heart, nurturing future leaders, empowering your team, and guiding them through challenges. Through your leadership, may you cultivate a culture of collaboration and unity, and may your journey be one of inspiration and transformation. As you ascend to new heights as a sales manager, may your legacy be one of empowerment, growth, and unwavering dedication to excellence.

Igniting Excellence: Motivating and Leading Sales Teams

In the bustling landscape of sales, where every interaction is a chance to create connections and achieve success, the role of a leader takes on a special significance. As you step into the realm of motivating and leading sales teams, you become the catalyst that transforms individual efforts into a collective force of achievement and inspiration.

The Flame of Motivation

Imagine a fire that burns with an unyielding intensity. Your role as a leader is akin to tending this fire of motivation within your team. Just as a flame needs fuel to stay alive, your team requires encouragement, recognition, and a clear vision to ignite their passion and keep it burning brightly.

Cultivating a Vision

Think of a skilled gardener nurturing seeds into flourishing plants. Your role is that of a visionary gardener, planting the seeds of purpose and direction in the hearts of your team members. With a compelling vision, you guide them towards a common goal, showing them not just the destination but the path to get there.

Leading by Example

Picture a trailblazer who forges a path through uncharted territory. As a leader, you are that trailblazer, setting the standard through your actions and dedication. Your commitment to excellence becomes a beacon that inspires your team to follow your lead and strive for greatness.

Nurturing Growth

Imagine a conductor harmonizing a symphony, each instrument contributing to a masterpiece. Your leadership orchestrates the talents of your team members into a symphony of success. By providing opportunities for growth, mentoring, and learning, you cultivate an environment where each member can reach their full potential.

Empowering Through Trust

Think of a captain at the helm of a ship, navigating through uncharted waters. In your leadership role, you are that captain, steering your team with trust and confidence. By empowering your team to take ownership of their tasks and decisions, you create an atmosphere where innovation and initiative flourish.

Fostering Collaboration

Envision a skilled architect designing a complex structure that relies on the strength of its foundation. In the realm of leading sales teams, you are that architect, building a foundation of collaboration and teamwork. Your ability to foster open communication and cooperation transforms individual efforts into a powerful collective force.

Recognizing Achievements

As you lead and motivate your sales team, remember that recognition is like sunlight for a plant—it nurtures growth. Celebrate the successes, both big and small, and acknowledge the hard work and dedication of your team. Your appreciation serves as fuel for their motivation, inspiring them to continue striving for excellence.

Crafting a Legacy of Inspiration

As a leader, you have the opportunity to craft a legacy of inspiration and impact. Your role extends beyond managing tasks; it's about empowering individuals to excel and fostering an environment where everyone thrives. Your guidance Molds the future of your team, shaping them into a force that drives innovation, resilience, and collective achievement.

Step into your role with passion, purpose, and dedication. Nourish the flame of motivation, cultivate a compelling vision, and lead by example. Your leadership empowers growth, fosters collaboration, and recognizes achievements. Through your guidance, may your sales team not only reach new heights of success but also become a beacon of inspiration for the wider world. May your journey be one of empowerment, growth, and the creation of a legacy that illuminates the path for generations to come.

Nurturing Brilliance: Coaching and Developing Sales Talent

In the vibrant tapestry of the sales landscape, coaching and developing sales talent is like tending to a garden of potential. As a seasoned leader, your role is not only to guide your team towards success but also to nurture their growth, allowing each member to flourish into their fullest potential.

The Role of a Coach

Imagine a coach on the sidelines of a game, shaping players into champions through guidance and support. As a sales leader, you step into this role, becoming a beacon of encouragement and a wellspring of wisdom. Your goal is to transform your team members into confident, skilled professionals who can navigate the complexities of the sales journey.

The Art of Feedback

Think of a sculptor carefully chiselling a block of marble to reveal a masterpiece within. Your feedback is the chisel that shapes your team's abilities, moulding them into refined instruments of success. Constructive feedback not only identifies areas for improvement but also provides a roadmap for growth.

Individualized Development Plans

Picture an architect crafting blueprints for a grand structure. Your role is to design individualized development plans that align with each team member's unique strengths and aspirations. By tailoring growth strategies, you empower individuals to enhance their skills and contribute to the collective success.

Creating a Learning Culture

Imagine a garden where diverse plants coexist and thrive. Your leadership creates a learning culture that embraces the exchange of ideas, experiences, and knowledge. By fostering an environment of continuous learning, you encourage your team to stay adaptable and open to new approaches in an ever-evolving field.

Mentoring and Role Modelling

Envision a lighthouse guiding ships safely through stormy seas. As a mentor and role model, your light illuminates the path for your team members, helping them navigate challenges and uncertainties. Through your own actions and experiences, you provide valuable insights and inspiration for their journey.

Empowerment Through Responsibility

Think of a conductor leading an orchestra, each member contributing to a symphony of success. Your leadership style empowers team members by delegating responsibility and ownership of projects. This sense of ownership fuels their motivation and fosters a sense of accountability.

Celebrating Milestones

Picture a celebratory gathering where achievements are acknowledged and celebrated. Just as every victory deserves recognition, your role is to acknowledge the milestones reached by your team members. By celebrating their successes, you create an environment that motivates and uplifts, inspiring them to aim even higher.

Investing in Growth

As a coach and developer of sales talent, remember that your investment today shapes the leaders of tomorrow. Your dedication to nurturing their abilities and fostering growth creates a ripple effect, not only within your team but across the organization. Through your guidance, you cultivate a legacy of brilliance that continues to thrive long after you've moved on.

Embrace your role as a coach with enthusiasm and a commitment to excellence. Provide constructive feedback, design personalized development plans, and create a learning culture that empowers your team. Through mentoring and role modelling, you guide them towards success while celebrating their achievements. Your investment in growth shapes not only your team's future but also the landscape of sales as a whole. May your journey as a coach be one of inspiration, empowerment, and the nurturing of brilliance that leaves an indelible mark on the world of sales.

Chapter 14. conquering the Summit: Managing Sales Challenges

In the dynamic world of sales, challenges are the mountains that stand between you and your goals. Like an intrepid explorer, you're equipped with the tools and knowledge to conquer these peaks and turn obstacles into opportunities. Welcome to the chapter dedicated to managing sales challenges, where we'll delve into the art of overcoming adversity and emerging stronger on the other side.

Embracing the Test of Resilience

Imagine a mountaineer ascending a steep slope, facing unpredictable weather and treacherous terrain. The challenges you encounter in sales are the tests that measure your resilience and determination. This chapter is your guidebook for navigating these tests and emerging victorious.

The Landscape of Challenges

Think of the sales journey as a rugged landscape, filled with both expected and unexpected challenges. From economic shifts to changing consumer preferences, each obstacle requires a strategic approach and a resilient spirit. By developing effective strategies, you equip yourself to navigate through even the most challenging terrain.

Turning Challenges into Opportunities

Picture an alchemist transforming base metals into precious gold. Just as alchemy turns adversity into riches, your role is to turn challenges into opportunities for growth and innovation. By reframing challenges as catalysts for change, you tap into your ability to adapt, innovate, and thrive.

The Power of Problem Solving

Envision a puzzle solver meticulously fitting pieces together to unveil a complete picture. As a sales professional, you're a master problem solver, capable of dissecting challenges, identifying root causes, and designing solutions. Your ability to approach challenges strategically enhances your effectiveness and influence.

Resilience and Adaptability

Imagine a tree bending and swaying with the force of the wind yet remaining firmly rooted. Resilience is your anchor during stormy times, allowing you to bend without breaking. With adaptability, you harness the power to pivot, evolve, and navigate even the most unexpected challenges.

Embracing Change as a Constant

Picture a river flowing through diverse landscapes, forever changing its course. Just as a river adapts to new terrains, your journey in sales requires embracing change as a constant companion. Your ability to adapt to evolving circumstances ensures that challenges are not roadblocks but steppingstones on your path to success.

The Mindset of a Champion

Think of a sports champion facing adversity during a match, driven by the determination to triumph. Your mindset in managing sales challenges is what propels you forward. By cultivating a growth mindset and a resolute attitude, you transform challenges into opportunities for personal and professional development.

Elevating Through Challenges

As you embark on this chapter, remember that each challenge is an invitation to elevate yourself to new heights. Embrace the tests of resilience, see challenges as opportunities for growth, and wield the power of problem-solving. By infusing your journey with adaptability and a champion's mindset, you ascend the peaks of sales challenges with grace and tenacity.

Equip yourself with the knowledge and strategies needed to conquer the landscape of sales challenges. Just as an explorer conquers mountains, you navigate obstacles and emerge stronger than before. May your journey through this chapter be one of enlightenment, empowerment, and the unwavering belief that challenges are the steppingstones to your ultimate success.

Navigating the Storm: Overcoming Sales Burnout and Rejection

In the realm of sales, where highs and lows are frequent companions, the journey can sometimes lead to exhaustion and frustration. Welcome to the chapter dedicated to handling sales burnout and rejection, where we delve into the art of maintaining your resilience, finding renewed motivation, and transforming setbacks into steppingstones.

The Pitfalls of Burnout

Imagine a fire burning too intensely, depleting its own fuel until it flickers out. Burnout is the consequence of relentless effort without replenishment. The demanding nature of the sales world, with its targets, quotas, and constant pressure, can lead to burnout. Recognizing the signs is the first step to regaining your balance.

Rejection: The Unwanted Companion

Think of rejection as a storm cloud casting a shadow over the sunniest of days. Just as every weather system eventually passes, rejection is part of the sales landscape. Whether it's a lost deal, an unresponsive prospect, or a difficult client, rejection can dent your confidence and enthusiasm. Learning to manage it is essential for your mental well-being.

Reframing Rejection

Imagine a painter turning a blank canvas into a masterpiece. Similarly, you can transform rejection into an opportunity for growth. Reframe each rejection as a chance to learn, adapt, and refine your approach. The lessons you gather from each setback become tools to shape your future success.

Caring for Your Mental Health

Think of yourself as a gardener tending to a delicate plant. Your mental health requires nourishment, care, and occasional pruning. Amidst the demands of sales, prioritizing self-care is non-negotiable. Regular exercise, mindfulness, and spending time with loved ones serve as your emotional anchors.

Cultivating Resilience

Imagine a tree bending gracefully with the wind but remaining steadfast in its roots. Resilience is your shield against the battering winds of burnout and rejection. By cultivating a resilient mindset, you bounce back stronger from setbacks. Embrace setbacks as temporary hurdles rather than permanent barriers.

Strategies for Recovery

Picture a traveller stopping at an oasis to rest, refresh, and gather strength. When burnout threatens to overwhelm you, take a step back. Reevaluate your priorities, set boundaries, and engage in activities that recharge your energy. Additionally, seek support from peers, mentors, and friends who understand the challenges of your journey.

The Power of Positivity

Think of positivity as a beacon that guides you through the darkest of nights. Maintaining a positive outlook is your anchor in turbulent times. Cultivate gratitude, celebrate small wins, and surround yourself with a network that uplifts and encourages you.

Transforming Rejection into Resilience

As you journey through this chapter, remember that sales burnout and rejection are part of the landscape. Just as a captain steers a ship through a storm, you navigate these challenges with skill and determination. By reframing rejection, nurturing your mental well-being, and cultivating resilience, you emerge not only stronger but also more compassionate and adaptable.

Equip yourself with the strategies to weather the storms of burnout and rejection. Just as a phoenix rises from the ashes, you transform setbacks into opportunities for growth. May your experience in this chapter be one of empowerment, enlightenment, and the unwavering belief that challenges are catalysts for your evolution.

Navigating the Battlefield: Conquering Price Objections and Competition

In the arena of sales, price objections and competition stand as formidable opponents on the path to success. Welcome to the chapter where we arm you with the strategies to face these challengers head-on, transforming them from barriers into steppingstones toward victory.

Price Objections: Unmasking the Challenge

Imagine a fortress guarding a hidden treasure. Price objections are the guardians, challenging your value proposition. When prospects raise concerns about cost, it's not just about the figures—it's a request for you to reveal the hidden gems within your offering.

The Art of Value Communication

Think of yourself as a storyteller, painting a vivid picture of the benefits your product or service brings. Effective value communication goes beyond numbers. It's about showcasing how your solution meets their needs, solves their problems, and ultimately enhances their lives or businesses.

Addressing Price Concerns with Confidence

Picture a skilled diplomat navigating a delicate negotiation. Addressing price objections requires finesse and empathy. Listen carefully to your prospect's concerns, acknowledge their perspective, and then guide them toward understanding the total value they're gaining, which often far outweighs the cost.

Showcasing ROI and Long-Term Benefits

Imagine a garden where diligent planting yields abundant harvests. Your solution is that seed of prosperity. Shift the focus from immediate cost to long-term benefits. Illustrate how your product's impact can lead to cost savings, improved efficiency, or increased revenue, justifying the investment.

The Dance of Competition

Think of the sales landscape as a dance floor, with competitors as your partners. Embrace competition as an opportunity for growth. Instead of viewing competitors as threats, see them as benchmarks that push you to innovate and differentiate.

Showcasing Unique Value

Imagine you're an artist creating a masterpiece. Your product or service is your canvas, and your unique value proposition is the brushstroke that sets you apart. Highlight what makes your offering distinct—whether it's superior quality, exceptional customer service, or innovative features.

Turning Competitors into Allies

Picture a relay race where each team member contributes their strengths. Forge partnerships with prospects that align better with your competitors. Be candid about your strengths and acknowledge your limitations. Sometimes, referring prospects to your competitors with grace can build goodwill.

Equipped for Victory

As you delve into this chapter, remember that price objections and competition are not insurmountable foes. By mastering the art of value communication, addressing price concerns with confidence, showcasing ROI, and embracing competition as a catalyst for growth, you equip yourself for triumph.

Transform these challenges into opportunities to showcase your prowess. Just as a skilled craftsman shapes raw materials into a masterpiece, you shape objections and competition into steppingstones toward success. May your journey through this chapter be one of empowerment, enlightenment, and the unwavering belief that every challenge is a chance for you to shine.

Navigating the Seas of Change: Adapting to Market Shifts and Industry Trends

Welcome to the section where we set sail on the ever-changing seas of the market, exploring how to navigate the currents of transformation and ride the waves of evolving industry trends. In this journey, you'll learn how to not just survive but thrive in the face of change.

The Winds of Change: Market Shifts

Imagine you're a seasoned sailor navigating your ship through turbulent waters. Just as the wind can shift suddenly, so can the market dynamics. Economic shifts, technological advancements, and unforeseen events can all alter the landscape you're operating in.

Embracing the Agile Mindset

Picture a dancer moving gracefully to a changing rhythm. An agile mindset is your dance partner when the music changes. Embrace flexibility and open-mindedness. Be ready to adjust your strategies and adapt your approach as market conditions transform.

The Beacon of Industry Trends

Think of yourself as an explorer in uncharted territories. Industry trends act as beacons, guiding your ship toward new horizons. Staying informed about emerging technologies, consumer preferences, and market shifts allows you to anticipate change and position yourself accordingly.

The Art of Pivoting

Imagine an artist skilfully transforming their canvas mid-stroke. When market shifts occur, consider it an opportunity to pivot. Assess how your product or service aligns with the changing needs and desires of your target audience. Adapt your offerings to remain relevant and valuable.

Strategies for Riding the Waves

Think of yourself as a surfer, riding the crests of industry trends. To master the art of adaptation, stay curious and be a lifelong learner. Attend industry events, read relevant publications, and engage in conversations with thought leaders. These actions will empower you to anticipate change and ride the waves of innovation.

The Power of Customer Feedback

Imagine you're a sculptor shaping a masterpiece based on feedback. Your customers are your guides in this journey. Listen attentively to their needs, concerns, and preferences. Incorporate their insights into your strategies, ensuring that your offerings remain aligned with their evolving requirements.

Setting Your Sail for Success

As you navigate this page, remember that adapting to market changes and industry trends is not a sign of weakness but a display of resilience and foresight. By embracing an agile mindset, staying informed about trends, pivoting when necessary, and leveraging customer feedback, you set your sail for success.

Just as a skilled navigator adjusts the course to reach their destination, you adjust your strategies to thrive amidst change. May this page inspire you to view market shifts as opportunities and industry trends as guides. As you venture forth into this dynamic landscape, know that your ability to adapt is your strongest asset. May your journey be one of constant growth, exploration, and the discovery of new horizons.

Chapter 15. Pioneering Tomorrow: Unveiling the Future of Sales and Emerging Trends

Welcome to the chapter that shines a spotlight on the horizon of sales, where we peer into the crystal ball of innovation and explore the exciting world of emerging trends. In this expedition, we'll unravel the mysteries of the future and equip you with insights to boldly stride into uncharted territory.

The Winds of Change: A Glimpse into Tomorrow

Imagine standing on the precipice of a new era, feeling the winds of change brushing against your face. The future of sales is a landscape in constant flux, shaped by technology, shifting consumer behaviours, and evolving market dynamics. To navigate this uncharted territory, we must embrace the spirit of pioneers.

Technological Revolution: Embracing the Digital Frontier

Visualize a tapestry woven with the threads of innovation. The digital age has revolutionized the way we interact and conduct business. From AI-powered chatbots to data-driven insights, technology is your compass in this new terrain. As a salesperson, embracing these tools empowers you to anticipate customer needs and personalize experiences.

Customer-Centric Universe: The Rise of Empathy

Imagine walking in your customer's shoes, understanding their journey intimately. The future of sales revolves around empathetic engagement. Customers demand personalized experiences and authentic connections.

This means understanding their pain points, tailoring solutions, and building relationships that withstand the test of time.

Sustainability and Social Responsibility: A New Ethical Frontier

Picture a world where every transaction carries a trace of social good. The future of sales transcends profit and embraces purpose. Sustainability and social responsibility are no longer buzzwords but guiding principles. Businesses that align with ethical values and contribute positively to society will shine brightly in this new era.

The Art of Data Mastery: Unveiling Insights

Imagine gazing into a starlit sky, each star a data point waiting to be deciphered. The future of sales is driven by data mastery. Analytics and insights illuminate the path ahead, guiding your decisions and strategies. By understanding customer behaviour and trends, you'll wield the power to anticipate market shifts and lead the way.

Human Touch in a Digital World: A Harmonious Symphony

Visualize a symphony where technology and the human touch dance in harmony. The future of sales marries digital efficiency with the warmth of personal connection. As automation handles routine tasks, you're free to invest your energy in building meaningful relationships and delivering exceptional value.

Charting Your Course to Tomorrow

As you embark on this chapter, remember that the future of sales is an ever-evolving canvas waiting for your brushstrokes. Embrace technology, cultivate empathy, champion sustainability, and harness the power of data. By doing so, you become a beacon of innovation, a harbinger of positive change.

Just as an explorer sets sail to new continents, you set forth into the future of sales, driven by curiosity and a pioneering spirit. May this chapter ignite your imagination and fuel your determination to shape the future. As you journey through emerging trends, know that you are not just a passenger; you are the captain of your destiny. May your sails be filled with innovation, and may your course be guided by purpose and prosperity.

Elevating Sales Through AI and Automation

Welcome to the realm where technology meets human ingenuity in the world of sales. In this section, we'll embark on a journey into the future, exploring how AI and automation are reshaping the landscape of sales, empowering professionals like you to achieve greater heights.

The Dawn of AI: Enhancing Efficiency and Insight

Imagine having a trusted assistant who anticipates your every need. AI is that partner. Artificial Intelligence has revolutionized sales by streamlining processes, crunching data, and unveiling insights that were once hidden. It's like a compass guiding you to the heart of your customers' desires.

Personalization Redefined: Crafting Tailored Experiences

Visualize walking into a tailor's shop, and the tailor already knows your exact measurements. AI offers that level of personalization in sales. By analysing customer data, it creates individualized experiences that resonate with the unique preferences of each prospect. With AI, every interaction feels like it was made just for them.

Sifting Through the Data: Unveiling Actionable Insights

Picture a treasure chest of insights waiting to be discovered. AI doesn't just gather data; it interprets it. It pinpoints trends, deciphers patterns, and forecasts future behaviours. This empowers you to make informed decisions, predict market shifts, and design strategies that are ahead of the curve.

Automating the Routine: Liberation Through Efficiency

Imagine having more time for what truly matters. Automation takes care of repetitive tasks, liberating you from the mundane. From sending follow-up emails to updating CRM records, automation ensures that your focus is directed towards high-impact activities that demand your creativity and expertise.

The Power of Predictive Analytics: Anticipating Needs

Visualize knowing what a customer needs before they even express it. AI-powered predictive analytics are your crystal ball. They analyse past behaviours to forecast future actions. Armed with these insights, you can proactively offer solutions, delighting customers by meeting their needs before they arise.

Building Stronger Relationships: A Human-AI Symphony

Imagine a symphony where AI plays alongside the human touch. AI doesn't replace you; it augments you. It provides the information you need to establish authentic connections, fuel meaningful conversations, and address pain points. AI becomes your assistant, allowing you to focus on the art of building relationships.

Charting the Future with AI and Automation

As you delve into this section, remember that AI and automation are tools, and you are the master craftsman. Embrace their capabilities and harness their potential. By doing so, you elevate your sales game, create unforgettable customer experiences, and unlock new realms of productivity.

You stand at the crossroads of tradition and innovation, where the art of sales converges with the power of technology. Like a painter using new colours on an age-old canvas, you'll weave AI and automation into your sales journey, creating a masterpiece that captures the hearts of your clients. May this section inspire you to embrace the future, leveraging AI and automation to sculpt a path that leads not just to success, but to a symphony of human connection and technological marvel.

Personalization: The Heartbeat of Customer-Centric Selling

In the realm of sales, every interaction is an opportunity to create a connection that resonates deeply with your customers. Welcome to the world of personalization and customer-centric selling, where each prospect is treated as an individual, and every touchpoint is a chance to craft an experience that leaves an indelible mark.

The Power of the Personal Touch

Imagine walking into a café, and the barista greets you by name, already knowing your favourite brew. Personalization in sales is akin to that warm greeting. It's about acknowledging that your customers aren't just numbers; they are unique individuals with distinct preferences, needs, and pain points.

Understanding the Customer's Universe

Picture yourself as an explorer of your customer's universe. Delve into their journey, comprehend their challenges, and grasp their aspirations. By immersing yourself in their world, you gain insights that allow you to tailor your approach, making your interactions not just transactions, but meaningful connections.

Crafting Bespoke Experiences

Visualize being a tailor, creating bespoke suits that fit perfectly. In customer-centric selling, you craft experiences that fit perfectly into your client's world. Whether it's a personalized email, a recommendation based on their history, or an understanding of their timeline, each touchpoint showcases your commitment to addressing their specific needs.

Data as the Brushstroke of Personalization

Imagine having a palette of colours that captures the essence of your customer's preferences. Data is your palette, allowing you to paint intricate portraits of your clients. By analysing their past interactions, behaviours, and feedback, you can predict what they want even before they do.

Building Relationships Through Empathy

Picture yourself in your customer's shoes, experiencing their challenges firsthand. Empathy is the cornerstone of personalization. By stepping into their world and acknowledging their struggles, you foster a relationship built on trust, showing that you genuinely care about their success.

The Dance of Balance: Automation and Human Touch

Visualize a dance where automation and human touch intertwine seamlessly. Personalization doesn't mean sacrificing efficiency. With the help of technology, you can scale personalization while maintaining the human element. It's a harmonious dance that ensures each customer feels valued, no matter the scale.

The Symphony of Delight: A Customer-Centric Future

As you delve into this section, remember that personalization and customer-centric selling are about more than just closing deals. They are about creating experiences that resonate long after the transaction is complete. By putting your customers at the centre of your universe, you craft a symphony of delight that leaves them not just satisfied, but eager to return.

You stand at the crossroads of tradition and innovation, where the essence of personal connection meets the power of data-driven insights. Like a sculptor moulding clay, you'll shape your sales approach to fit the contours of your customers' needs. May this section inspire you to create a future where every interaction is a note in the melody of customer satisfaction, and each touchpoint is a brushstroke in the masterpiece of personalization and customer-centric excellence.

Predictive Analytics: Illuminating the Path of Data-Driven Sales

Welcome to the realm where crystal balls are replaced by algorithms, and insights are gleaned not from star patterns but from data patterns. This is the world of predictive analytics and data-driven sales, where every piece of information becomes a guiding star in your pursuit of success.

The Data Goldmine

Imagine yourself as a prospector in the digital age, searching not for gold nuggets but for nuggets of information. Predictive analytics is your treasure map, guiding you to the hidden gems buried within your data. It's about extracting valuable insights from the vast sea of information at your fingertips.

Foreseeing the Future with Data

Picture yourself as a modern-day oracle, deciphering cryptic messages in data sets. Predictive analytics allows you to gaze into the future with confidence, understanding customer behaviours before they even happen. By recognizing patterns and trends, you can anticipate needs, preferences, and potential pitfalls.

From Reactive to Proactive

Visualize a ship captain navigating through a stormy sea, using a compass to steer clear of danger. Predictive analytics is your compass, helping you navigate the turbulent waters of the market. Instead of reacting to challenges, you'll be equipped to proactively address them, ensuring smooth sailing toward your goals.

Personalization Perfected

Imagine a tailor with a magic measuring tape that predicts your clothing preferences. Predictive analytics is your magic tape, enabling you to tailor your approach with precision. By understanding your customer's preferences, you can create personalized experiences that feel like they were tailor-made for them.

Decoding the Customer's Mind

Picture yourself as a detective, piecing together clues to unravel a mystery. With predictive analytics, you become a detective of customer intent. By analysing their online behaviours, past purchases, and interactions, you uncover the hidden motivations that guide their decisions.

A Symphony of Insights

Visualize a symphony orchestra, where each instrument contributes to the harmonious whole. Predictive analytics is the conductor, orchestrating insights from various data sources into a symphony of actionable intelligence. From demographics to purchase history, every note plays a role in creating a coherent melody of strategy.

The Vision of Tomorrow: A Data-Driven Odyssey

As you delve into this section, remember that predictive analytics and data-driven sales aren't just about interpreting data points; they are about unravelling stories hidden within numbers. Like an artist with a palette, you'll use data to paint a picture of your customers' journeys. With every analysis, you'll be charting a course toward a future where decisions are guided by insights, and success is illuminated by data's guiding light.

You stand at the crossroads of tradition and innovation, where gut feelings meet data-backed decisions. As you explore the world of predictive analytics, may you uncover gems of knowledge that lead you toward a horizon of informed strategies and prosperous outcomes. May this section inspire you to embrace data as a compass, and predictive analytics as your guide on the exhilarating journey of data-driven sales.

16. Conclusion: Embracing the Mastery of Sales

Here, at the culmination of your journey, you stand not just as a sales professional, but as a master of the art of sales. Like an artisan who has honed their craft through dedication and passion, you have embarked on a transformative odyssey, and the treasures you've gained are not material but intellectual, emotional, and professional.

A Symphony of Skills

Imagine a symphony hall filled with the resonating harmonies of diverse instruments. Your journey in mastering the art of sales is like conducting this symphony. Each chapter, each skill you've cultivated, adds another layer of depth to the melody. From the crescendo of effective communication to the gentle cadence of relationship-building, you've orchestrated a masterpiece of sales prowess.

The Canvas of Possibilities

Picture yourself as an artist, standing before a canvas stretched wide with possibilities. Throughout this guide, you've painted your story with vibrant strokes of knowledge, inspiration, and technique. You've embraced the challenge of each brushstroke, transforming blank spaces into portraits of resilience, innovation, and growth.

A Continuous Symphony

Visualize a never-ending symphony, where each note seamlessly flows into the next. Your journey doesn't end here; it continues as a perpetual symphony of improvement and innovation. As the sales landscape evolves, you'll adapt and lead the melody of change, applying your mastery to new challenges, opportunities, and trends.

The Legacy of Mastery

Picture yourself as a guardian of ancient wisdom, passing down the secrets of your craft to the next generation. As you conclude this journey, you become part of a legacy, a lineage of skilled professionals who have woven their mark into the tapestry of the sales world. Your mastery isn't just for your own success; it's a gift to those who follow.

Stepping into the Future

Imagine standing on the cusp of a new day, the sun rising on an ever-evolving horizon. With each chapter you've embraced, you've taken a step forward into the future of sales. As you move forward, remember that mastery isn't about reaching a destination; it's about embracing the journey, the challenges, the triumphs, and the growth.

With each new day, you embark on a fresh canvas to paint your sales journey. As you conclude this guide, may you carry the wisdom of each chapter with you, infusing every interaction with the brilliance of your learning. Your journey continues, a symphony of expertise, innovation, and success. May the future unfold before you with boundless opportunities and may your mastery of the art of sales guide you toward unparalleled achievement and fulfilment.

Overview of Learnings: Navigating the Realm of Sales

In the immersive pages of this comprehensive guide, you have embarked on a transformative journey through the intricate world of sales. From the initial spark of curiosity to the mastery of the art, every chapter has unveiled invaluable insights, techniques, and wisdom that should now be etched into your professional repertoire.

Mastering the Craft:

At the heart of this journey lies the art of sales, a symphony of skills that orchestrate success. From effective communication and active listening to crafting compelling presentations and closing deals with finesse, you have uncovered the foundational elements that drive the sales process.

Nurturing Relationships:

The essence of sales lies in forging connections, and you have explored the power of cultivating relationships. By understanding customer needs, addressing pain points, and delivering exceptional service, you've learned that sales extend far beyond transactions, shaping long-lasting partnerships and loyalty.

Navigating Challenges:

In the realm of sales, challenges are inevitable, but you are now equipped with strategies to overcome them. Whether handling objections, managing rejection, or adapting to market shifts, you've discovered that resilience and creativity are your allies in the face of adversity.

Mastery and Leadership:

As the journey unfolds, you have transformed into a master of your craft, poised to lead and inspire others. With the art of sales under your belt, we've explored coaching, team management, and the transition from salesperson to sales manager, becoming a beacon of knowledge and guidance.

Emerging Horizons:

As the guide concludes, you can glimpse the future of sales, where AI, personalization, and data-driven insights pave the way for innovation. The journey's end is just the beginning of a perpetual symphony, as you step forward as torchbearers of change, embracing new trends and challenges with the wisdom you've cultivated.

A Continual Symphony:

This guide, like a symphony, is a compilation of harmonious chapters that crescendo into a masterful composition of knowledge and inspiration. With each turn of the page, you should have absorbed not just information, but a mindset that resonates with dedication, resilience, and the pursuit of excellence.

As you close this book, step into a world brimming with opportunities. The journey through these chapters has helped craft you into sales virtuoso, ready to seize the challenges and triumphs that lie ahead. Armed with the wisdom, insights, and expertise gained from these pages, you can embark on a boundless adventure, ready to create your own symphony of success in the realm of sales.

www.ingramcontent.com/pod-product-compliance
Lightning Source LLC
Chambersburg PA
CBHW062331290526
45794CB00005B/1989